Regular Expression Recipes:
A Problem-Solution Approach

NATHAN A. GOOD

Apress®

Regular Expression Recipes: A Problem-Solution Approach

Copyright © 2005 by Nathan A. Good

ISBN-13 (pbk): 978-1-59059-441-4
ISBN-10 (pbk): 1-59059-441-X
Printed and bound in the United States of America 9 8 7 6 5 4 3 2

Lead Editor: Chris Mills
Technical Reviewer: Bill Johnson
Editorial Board: Steve Anglin, Dan Appleman, Ewan Buckingham, Gary Cornell, Tony Davis,
    Jason Gilmore, Chris Mills, Dominic Shakeshaft, Jim Sumser
Project Manager: Tracy Brown Collins
Copy Edit Manager: Nicole LeClerc
Copy Editor: Kim Wimpsett
Production Manager: Kari Brooks-Copony
Production Editor: Ellie Fountain
Compositor: Dina Quan
Proofreader: Linda Marousek
Cover Designer: Kurt Krames
Manufacturing Manager: Tom Debolski

Distributed to the book trade in the United States by Springer-Verlag New York, Inc., 233 Spring Street, 6th Floor, New York, NY 10013, and outside the United States by Springer-Verlag GmbH & Co. KG, Tiergartenstr. 17, 69112 Heidelberg, Germany.

In the United States: phone 1-800-SPRINGER, fax 201-348-4505, e-mail orders@springer-ny.com, or visit http://www.springer-ny.com. Outside the United States: fax +49 6221 345229, e-mail orders@springer.de, or visit http://www.springer.de.

For information on translations, please contact Apress directly at 2560 Ninth Street, Suite 219, Berkeley, CA 94710. Phone 510-549-5930, fax 510-549-5939, e-mail info@apress.com, or visit http://www.apress.com.

The source code for this book is available to readers at http://www.apress.com in the Source Code section.

Contents at a Glance

Contents

About the Author

■**NATHAN A. GOOD** lives in the Twin Cities area in Minnesota. As a contractor, he does software development, software architecture, and systems administration for a variety of companies.

When he is not writing software, Nathan enjoys building PCs and servers, reading about and working with new technologies, and trying to get all of his friends to make the move to open source software. When he's not at a computer, he spends time with his family, his church, and at the movies.

About the Technical Reviewer

Having worked as a computer consultant, independent contractor, and an IT employee, **BILL JOHNSON** has developed a strong background in many areas, including information systems technologies, system administration, application development, web development and deployment, game research and development, and graphics manipulation. Bill operates as a full-time consultant, and at the same time continues to play his role as one of four active shareholders/board members for a successful computer consulting company based in Bloomington, Minnesota. He is currently involved in maintaining numerous servers, Web sites, and office networks for a variety of clients, both professional and personal.

Bill graduated summa cum laude from Bemidji State University with a bachelor's degree in computer science. He has earned his private pilot instrument license and is a certified SCUBA diver. As well as serving on the Jordan Community Education advisory board, he also enjoys coaching his two boys in various athletic programs, karate, hiking, camping, fishing, and hunting. Bill may be contacted at review@katr.com.

Acknowledgments

I would like to first of all thank God. I would also like to thank my wonderful and supportive wife and kids for being patient and sacrificing while I was working on this book. I couldn't have done this work if it wasn't for my wonderful parents and grandparents.

Also, I would like to thank Jeffrey E. F. Friedl for his stellar book, *Mastering Regular Expressions* (both editions).

Introduction

This book contains recipes for regular expressions. It provides ready-to-go, real-world implementations and explains the expressions in detail. The approach is right to the point, and it will get you up and using regular expressions quickly.

Who Should Read This Book

This book was written for Web and application programmers and developers who might need to use regular expressions in their applications, but don't have the time to become entrenched in the details. While the recipes in this book are explained thoroughly, and you can get a very good understanding of how regular expressions work from them, you can also use the recipes as is, without having to know exactly how they work.

This book was also written for people who don't know they should use regular expressions yet. It provides many common tasks that can be done in other ways besides using regular expressions, but that could be made simpler using regular expressions. Many methods that use more than one replacement method can be rewritten as one regular expression replacement.

Finally, this book was written for programmers who have some spare time and want to quickly pick up something new to impress their friends or the cute COBOL developer down the hall. Perhaps you're in an office where regular expressions are regarded as voodoo magic—cryptic incantations that everyone fears and nobody understands. This is your chance to become the Grand Wizard of Expressions, to be revered by your peers.

This book does not provide an exhaustive explanation of how regular expression engines read expressions or do matches. Also, this book does not cover advanced regular expression techniques such as optimization. Some of the expressions in this book have been written to be easy to read and use, at the expense of some performance. If those topics are of interest to you, see *Mastering Regular Expressions* by Jeffrey E. F. Friedl (O'Reilly, 1997).

Conventions Used in This Book

Throughout this book, changes in typeface and type weight will let you know if I am referring to a regular expression recipe or a string. The example code given in recipes is in a fixed-width font like this:

```
This is sample code.
```

The actual expression in the recipe is called out in bold type:

```
Here is an expression.
```

When expressions and the strings they might match are listed in text, they look like this.

Related recipes, which are recipes that are similar because they use the same metacharacters or character sequences, are listed like this at the end of each recipe:

▮**See Also** 4-9, 5-1

How This Book Is Organized

This book is split into sets of examples called *recipes*. The recipes contain expressions to do the same task, like replacing words. In each recipe, there are examples in Perl, PHP, and/or Python, Vim, and common Unix shell commands like sed and grep.

After each recipe, a section called "How It Works" breaks the example down and tells you why the expression works. The expression is explained character by character, with text explanations of each character or metacharacter. When I was first learning regular expressions, it was useful to me to read the expression out loud while I was going through it. Don't worry about your co-workers looking at you oddly—the minute you begin wielding the awesome power of regular expressions, the joke will be on them.

After the examples, near the end of some of the recipes, is a section called "Variations." This section highlights some common variations of expressions used in some of the recipes.

The code samples in this book in Perl, PHP, and Python are very simple, and are, for the most part, identical for two reasons. First, each example is ready to use and complete enough to show the expression working. Second, at the same time, the focus of these examples is the expression, not the code.

The recipes are split into common tasks, such as working with CSV and tab-delimited files, or working with source code. The recipes are not organized from simple to more difficult, as there is little point in trying to rate expressions in their difficulty level. The tasks are as follows:

- *Words and text*: These recipes introduce many concepts in expressions, but also show common tasks used in replacing and searching for words and text in regular blocks of text.

- *URLs and paths*: These recipes are useful when operating on filenames, file paths, and URLs.

- *CSV and tab-delimited files*: These recipes show how to change CSV records to tab-delimited records, and how to perform tasks such as extracting single fields from tab-delimited records.

- *Formatting and validating*: These recipes are useful for writing formatting and validation routines in applications where the data is widely varying user input.

- *HTML and XML*: These recipes provide examples for working with HTML and XML files, such as removing HTML attributes and finding HTML attributes.

- *Coding and using the command line*: This final group of recipes shows expressions that can be used to find text within comments or perform replacements on parameters.

What Regular Expressions Are

If you know any mathematical expressions, you already know basically what regular expressions are. Regular expressions are just like mathematical expressions, except they operate on sequences of characters, or *strings*, instead of numbers.

Understanding this concept will help you understand the best way to learn how to use regular expressions. Chances are, when you see 4 + 3 = 7, you *think* "four plus three equals seven." The goal of this book is to duplicate that thought process in the "How It Works" sections, where expressions are broken down into single characters and explained. An expression such as ^$ becomes "the beginning of a line followed immediately by the end of a line."

Regular expressions can be very concise, considering how much they can say. Their brevity has the benefit of allowing you to say quite a lot with one small, well-written expression. However, a drawback of this brevity is that regular expressions can be very difficult to read, especially if you're the poor developer picking up someone else's uncommented work. Expressions like ^['][^']*?'[^']*?' can be difficult to debug if you don't know what the author was trying to do or why the author was doing it that way. Although this is a problem in all code that is not thoroughly documented, the concise nature of expressions and the inability to debug them make the problem worse. Expressions can be commented, but realistically that isn't common.

What Regular Expressions Aren't

As I mentioned previously, regular expressions aren't easy to read or debug. They can easily lead to unexpected results because one misplaced character can change the entire meaning of the expression. Mismatched parentheses or quotes can cause major issues, and many syntax-highlighting IDEs that parse languages do nothing to help isolate these in regular expressions.

Regular expressions aren't used by everyone. With the advent of regular expression support in some really common languages (consider the RegularExpressionValidator in ASP.NET), I expect more and more people will begin using them. Just like anything else, be prudent and consider the skill set of those around you when doing the expressions. If you're working with a staff unfamiliar with regular expressions, make sure to comment your code until it's painfully obvious exactly what's going on.

When to Use Regular Expressions

Use regular expressions whenever there are rules with your string finding or replacement. Rules might be "Replace this, but only when it's at the beginning of a word" or "Find this, but only when it's inside parentheses." Regular expressions provide the opportunity for searches and replacements to be really intelligent and have a lot of logic packed into a relatively small space.

One of the most common places where I've used regular expressions is in "smart" interface validation. I've had clients with specific requests for U.S. postal codes, for instance. They wanted a five-number code like 55555 to work, but also a four-digit extension, such as 55555-4444. What's more, they wanted to allow the five- and four-digit groups to be separated by a dash, space, or nothing at all. As an expression, this is something that is fairly simple to do, but it takes more work in code using things like conditional statements based on the length of the string.

When Not to Use Regular Expressions

Don't use regular expressions when a simple search or replacement can be used with accuracy. If you intend to replace "moo" with "oink," and you don't care where the string is found, don't bother using an expression to do it. Instead, use the string method supported in the language you're using.

Consider *not* using expressions if in doing so it will take you longer to figure out the expression than to filter bad data by hand. For instance, if you know the data well enough that you already know you might only get three or four false matches that you can correct by hand in a few minutes, don't spend 15 minutes writing an expression. Of course, at some point you have to overcome a learning curve if you're new to expressions, so use your judgment. Just don't get too expression-happy for expressions' sake.

Syntax Overview

The following sections give an overview of the syntax of regular expressions as used in Perl, PHP, Python, Vim, grep, and sed. After reading this overview, you should be able to recognize characters and metacharacters in regular expressions and be able to build your own expressions.

Expression Parts

The terminology for various parts of expressions hasn't ever been as important to me as knowing how to use them. I'll touch briefly on some terminology that describes each part of an expression, and then get into how to put those parts together.

An expression can be either a single atom or the joining of more than one atom. An *atom* is a single character or a metacharacter. A *metacharacter* is a single character that has special meaning other than its literal meaning. An example of both an atom and a character is a; an example of both an atom and a metacharacter is ^ (a metacharacter that I'll explain in a minute). You put these atoms together to build an expression, like so: ^a.

You can put atoms into groups using parentheses, like so: (^a). Putting atoms in a group builds an expression that can be captured for back referencing, modified with a qualifier, or included in another group of expressions.

(starts a group of atoms.

)   ends a group of atoms.

Qualifiers

Qualifiers restrict the number of times the preceding expression may appear in a match. The common single-character qualifiers are ?, +, and *.

?   means "zero or one," which matches the preceding expression found zero or one times.

See Also   1-4, 2-3, 2-9, 2-11, 2-13, 2-14, 2-15, 4-1, 4-2, 4-10, 4-12, 4-13, 4-16, 4-17, 4-18, 4-21, 6-3

+   means "one or more." An expression using the + qualifier will match the previous expression one or more times, making it required but matching it as many times as possible.

■See Also 1-3, 1-14, 1-15, 2-7, 2-8, 2-10, 2-12, 2-13, 2-14, 3-1, 3-2, 3-3, 3-4, 3-5, 3-6, 4-4, 4-5, 4-7, 4-11, 4-19, 5-1, 5-2, 5-3, 5-7, 6-3, 6-10, 6-11, 6-12, 6-14, 6-15, 6-18, 6-19

* means "zero or more." You should use this qualifier carefully. Because it matches zero occurrences or the preceding expression, some unexpected results can occur.

■See Also 1-1, 1-7, 1-9, 1-15, 1-17, 1-25, 1-27, 2-2, 2-3, 2-4, 2-9, 3-6, 4-21, 6-2, 6-3, 6-4, 6-5, 6-10, 6-11, 6-12, 6-14, 6-15, 6-17, 6-20, 6-22

Ranges

Ranges, like qualifiers, specify the number of times a preceding expression can occur in the string. Ranges begin with { and end with }. Inside the brackets, either a single number or a pair of numbers can appear. A comma separates the pair of numbers.

When a single number appears in a range, it specifies how many times the preceding expression can appear. If commas separate two numbers, the first number specifies the least number of occurrences, and the second number specifies the most number of occurrences.

{ specifies the beginning of a range.

} specifies the end of a range.

$\{n\}$ specifies that the preceding expression is found n times.

$\{n,\}$ specifies that the preceding expression is found at least n times.

$\{n,m\}$ specifies that the preceding expression is found at least n but no more than m times.

Line Anchors

The ^ and $ metacharacters are line anchors. They match the beginning of the line and the end of the line, respectively, but they don't *consume* any real characters. When a match *consumes* a character, it means the character will be replaced by whatever is in the replacement expression. The fact that the line anchors don't match any real characters is important when making replacements because the replacement expression doesn't have to be written to put the ^ or $ back into the string.

^ specifies the beginning of the line.

$ specifies the end of the line.

An Escape

You can use the escape character \ to precede atoms that would otherwise be metacharacters but that need to be taken literally. The expression \+, for instance, will match + and doesn't mean \ is found one or many times.

\   indicates the escape character.

See Also 1-7, 1-18, 1-19, 2-1, 2-3, 2-4, 2-6, 2-7, 2-8, 2-9, 2-11, 2-12, 2-13, 2-14, 2-15, 3-1, 3-3, 3-5, 4-1, 4-2, 4-8, 4-10, 4-11, 4-12, 4-13, 4-16, 4-17, 4-20, 4-21, 5-1, 5-3, 5-4, 5-5, 5-6, 5-7, 6-1, 6-2, 6-3, 6-4, 6-5, 6-7, 6-8, 6-9, 6-10, 6-14, 6-15, 6-18, 6-20

Saying "or"

You use the | metacharacter as an or operator in regular expressions. You use it between expressions, which can consist of a single atom or an entire group.

| indicates or.

See Also 1-3, 1-16, 1-18, 2-1, 2-4, 2-6, 2-9, 2-11, 2-12, 3-1, 3-3, 3-5, 4-2, 4-10, 4-12, 4-16, 4-17, 5-1, 5-4, 6-1, 6-2, 6-8, 6-9, 6-14, 6-18

Character Classes

Character classes are defined by the square brackets [and], and they match a single character, no matter how many atoms are inside the character class. A sample character class is [ab], which will match *a* or *b*.

You can use the - character inside a character class to define a range of characters. For instance, [a-c] will match *a*, *b*, or *c*.

[indicates the beginning of a character class.

]   indicates the end of a character class.

To use the - character literally inside a character class, put it first. It's impossible for it to define a range if it's the first character in a range, so it's taken literally.

The ^ metacharacter, which normally is a line anchor that matches the beginning of a line, is a negation character when it's used as the first character inside a character class. If it isn't the first character inside the character class, it will be treated as a literal ^.

A character class also can be a sequence of a normal character preceded by an escape. One example is \s, which in Perl-Compatible Regular Expressions (PCREs) matches whitespace characters (either a tab or a space).

The character classes \t and \n are common examples found in nearly every implementation of regular expressions to match tabs and newline characters, respectively.

Matching Anything

The . character is a wildcard in regular expressions—it matches anything. Using .* will match anything, everything, or nothing.

   .   indicates any character.

▪**See Also** 2-4, 2-6, 2-7, 2-8, 2-9, 2-10, 2-11, 2-12, 3-5, 3-6, 4-1, 4-9, 4-19, 4-20, 4-21, 5-7, 6-2, 6-5, 6-8, 6-9, 6-10, 6-11, 6-12, 6-18, 6-19, 6-20, 6-21, 6-22

PCREs

PCREs are beefed up with many built-in character classes and additions to grouping functionality, as well as some advanced matching features. The "Advanced PCRE Features" section lists these in greater detail.

PCREs provide the ability to define groups that don't capture what they match. These are useful when using back references in replacements, because it's easier to keep track of back references if only the necessary expressions are grouped.

The sequence to open noncapturing parentheses in Perl is (?:. The closing is the same as a normal group:).

   (?:   indicates the beginning of a noncapturing group.

)   indicates the end of a noncapturing group.

Advanced PCRE Features

Look-arounds are advanced PCRE features that allow expressions to be used for matches without consuming any characters (much like how a line anchor works). Look-arounds are split into two categories: look-aheads and look-behinds.

Look-aheads search past the main expression to make sure whatever is defined in the look-ahead is either found (a positive look-ahead) or not found (a negative look-ahead).

   (?=   indicates the beginning of a positive look-ahead.

   (?!   indicates the beginning of a negative look-ahead.

)   indicates the end of either look-ahead.

Look-behinds search before an expression to see if whatever is defined in the look-behind can be found (a positive look-behind) or not found (a negative look-behind).

   (?<=   indicates the beginning of a positive look-behind.

   (?<!   indicates the beginning of a negative look-behind.

Comparisons

Table 1 compares the expressions for making matches. It's important to remember that with the GNU Not Unix (GNU) grep and Perl examples, you need to quote the expressions in the table. Since some of these characters also have special meanings in shells and programming languages, it's important to make that distinction. Most shells use single quotes as a way to tell the shell to not interpret characters found within the single quotes. In all the examples in this book, I use / as a delimiter in Perl.

Table 1. *Expressions for Matching*

How Do I Say . . .	In GNU grep?	In Perl?	In Vim?
The beginning of the line	^	^	^
The end of the line	$	$	$
One or more times	+	+	\+
At most one time	?	?	\? or \=
Zero or more	*	*	*
A group	(...)	(...)	\(...\)
A noncapturing group		(?:...)	\%(...\)
A tab	<tab>	\t	\t
A newline character	\n	\n	\n
A range	{n} or {n,m}	{n} or {n,m}	\{n} or \{n,m}
A character class	[...]	[...]	\[...\]
Any character	.	.	\.
Whitespace	[[:space:]]	\s	\s
A number	[[:digi:]] or [0-9]	\d	\d
A word boundary	\< or \>	\b	\< or \>
Or	|	|	\\|
An alphabetical character	[[:alpha:]] or [A-Za-z]	\	\a

Using Expressions in Perl

Perl offers really easy, short methods to gain access to regular expressions. Two operators, m and s, allow you to match and replace strings with regular expressions.

The m Operator

The following shows the syntax for comparing strings against regular expressions in Perl:

```
"Goodbye World!" =~ m/World/
```

Alternatively, you can use the following:

```
"Goodbye World!" =~ /World/
```

For brevity, I'll use the latter style in the recipes throughout this book.

The m operator is a conditional statement that you can use in an if block or a while loop. Although you can use any nonwhitespace or nonalphanumeric character as a delimiter with the m operator, in this book I'll use / as the delimiter. You can use a variable in place of the literal string, such as using $str instead of "Goodbye World!". The following is an example of printing a line that says Don't play with matches! when the match succeeds:

```
my $str = "Moo!  Oink!"; # assign the variable $str to a literal
if ( $str =~ m/Oink/ )
{
    print "Don't play with matches!";
}
```

The following alternative also works in a conditional statement:

```
my $str = "Moo!  Oink!"; # assign the variable $str to a literal
if ( $str =~ /Oink/ )
{
    print "Don't play with matches!";
}
```

The s Operator

The syntax for doing substitutions is to use the s operator, which is similar to the matching m operator shown previously. You also can use the s operator in a conditional statement, which will be true if you made a substitution. To simply assign a variable to the replaced string, use the following:

```
my $string = "My old string";
$string =~ s/old/new/;
print $string;
```

The previous code will print My new string.

To check to see if a substitution was made, just use the s operator as an evaluation, like so:

```
my $string = "My old string";
if ( $string =~ s/old/new/ )
{
    print $string;
}
```

This will also print My new string.

The substitution operator has a few modifiers that you'll see used throughout this book: e, g, i, m, o, s, and x. Table 2 lists the meanings of these modifiers.

Table 2. *Modifiers*

Modifier	What It Says
e	The right side is also a regular expression.
g	Make global replacements; replace all occurrences found.
i	Ignore the case in the matching pattern.
m	^ and $ match the newline \n (multiline searches).
o	Compile the pattern one time only, which is good for performance in loops.
s	Allow . to match the newline.
x	Ignore whitespace in the pattern (you can use this to put comments in your regular expression).

Using the Perl Examples in This Book

The Perl examples in this book are ready-to-go scripts that you can save and execute without any changes (most of the time). Of course, this assumes that Perl is installed on your system. You can find information about installing Perl at http://www.perl.org.

To run and execute an example on a Unix or Linux system, first save the code in the example to a file. After saving the file, make sure the file is executable by using chmod, as follows, where you can replace recipe1-1.pl with the name you've used for the example:

```
$ chmod 755 recipe1-1.pl
```

For more information about using chmod, see the online manual pages for chmod by typing the following at the command line:

```
$ man chmod
```

For Windows installations, you'll most likely run the script by typing the following:

```
> perl recipe1-1.pl
```

Before running the script, also verify that the location of the Perl interpreter is correct. In all the examples given in the recipes in this book, that location is /usr/bin/perl. If your location is different, such as /bin/perl or /usr/local/bin/perl, you'll need to update the example before you can execute it.

Once the file is executable and the interpreter has been pointed to the correct location, run the script by typing the following, where recipe1-1.pl is the name of the script:

```
$ ./recipe1-1.pl
```

You can also run the script by using Perl, like so:

```
$ perl recipe1-1.pl
```

Using Expressions in PHP

PHP provides two ways of searching and replacing with regular expressions. One of them is to use the ereg() and ereg_replace() methods, which use Portable Operating System Interface (POSIX) regular expressions. The other is to use the preg_match() and preg_replace() methods, which use PCREs for expressions. Using the PCREs is preferred, because they offer so many features over the POSIX regular expressions.

ereg() and eregi()

The ereg() method accepts the regular expression and the string to search as arguments.

```
ereg( 'SEARCH', $inmystring )
```

It evaluates to true if the match is found, so you can use it inside if statements and while loops to control flow.

```
if ( ereg( 'FIND', $needleinahaystack ) )
{
    print "Success!";
}
```

The eregi() method is a case-insensitive alternative.

ereg_replace()

The ereg_replace() method also uses POSIX regular expressions. It takes the expression, replacement expression, and string as arguments.

```
$mynewstring = ereg_replace( 'SEARCH', 'REPLACE', $inmystring )
```

preg_match()

The preg_match() method takes two to three parameters: the regular expression, the string to search, and, optionally, a variable that holds the array of matches found.

```
preg_match( '/FIND/', $mystr )
```

Alternatively, you could use the following:

```
preg_match( '/FIND/', $mystr, $matchArray )
```

Notice that the regular expressions in the first parameter must start and end with a delimiter, just like the Perl expressions.

preg_replace()

The preg_replace() method accepts the regular expression for searching, the expression for the replacement, and the variable containing the string to replace. The preg_replace() method returns the new string with the replacements made. The following is an example of using preg_replace():

```
$newstring = preg_replace( '/OLD/', 'NEW', $original )
```

The PCREs in preg_replace support back references in the replacement by using \1 to access the first group, \2 to access the second group, and so on.

Using the PHP Examples in This Book

You need to put the PHP examples in this book in a location that's accessible by a Web server. Usually this is a directory under a document root defined by the Web server or a published directory under a user's home directory. In either case, you need to save the PHP examples as files that can be read by the Web server. I use mod_php with the Apache Web server for my PHP development, which is probably the most common way to expose PHP pages to the Internet.

Also, the PHP examples require that a PHP module be installed and used by the Web server. Setting up a PHP engine to work with a Web server is beyond the scope of this book, but you can find more information at http://www.php.net.

After you've saved the files in a location that's accessible by the Web server, you can run the examples by browsing to their location on your computer by opening a Web browser and typing something such as http://localhost/ch1/recipe1-1.php if the file recipe1-1.php is saved in a directory called ch1 directly under the Web server's document root.

Using Expressions in Python

To use regular expressions in Python, you must import the re module in the script. Use the raw-string syntax r'' when using regular expressions so you don't have to escape all the backslashes.

match()

Compile a regular expression with the re.compile() method, and then you can call the match() method to see if a string matches the expression.

```
import re
regex = re.compile( r'SEARCH' )
if regex.match( "My string here" ):
    print "No match",
```

sub()

The replacement method in the Python re module is sub(). The sub() method accepts the replacement string, the string in which to make the replacement, and optionally a count that specifies the number of times to make the replacement. If nothing is specified for the last parameter, the replacement is made as many times as possible.

The sub() method returns a copy of the second parameter with the replacements made.

```
import re
regex = re.compile( r'SEARCH' )
if regex.sub( r'REPLACE', mystr ):
    print "No match"
```

Using the Python Examples in This Book

The Python examples in this book require Python to be installed on your system. You can read about Python installation and get the Python installation files from http://www.python.org.

To execute a Python example, save the example in a file and make sure the location of the interpreter is correct. In this book, the location of the interpreter is /usr/bin/python. If the interpreter is in a different location, such as /bin/python or /usr/local/bin/python, update the example to include the appropriate location.

Once you've saved the file and the location of interpreter is correct, make sure the file is executable by using chmod in the Unix and Linux environments:

```
$ chmod 755 recipe1-1.py
```

or call the Python interpreter on the command line, and pass the name of the file to the interpreter as an argument:

```
$ python recipe1-1.py
```

Using Expressions in Vim

To search for a string in Vim, press the / key and type the expression while you're not in edit mode. The first string after the position of the cursor will be found. To navigate to the next result, press the n key.

To make replacements in Vim, use the s command, like so:

```
:s/OLD/NEW/
```

The previous command will make the replacement on the current line. To make a replacement on more than one line, you can specify the line numbers before the s command, or use % to make the replacements on all the lines in the file. The following example makes the replacement on lines 1 through 5:

```
:1,5s/NEW/OLD/
```

Use $ to specify the last line in the file without having to know the exact line number. The following is an example of making a replacement from line 20 to the end of the file:

```
:20,$s/NEW/OLD/
```

These examples will replace only the first occurrence found on each line. To match all the occurrences on each line, use the g option with the search, like so:

```
:%s/OLD/NEW/g
```

Using the Vim Examples in This Book

The Vim examples in this book are ready to be used as search or replacement commands in Vim. You can enter them when Vim isn't in edit mode.

Using Expressions with GNU grep

The version of grep that's shown in examples throughout this book is GNU grep. GNU grep accepts a POSIX regular expression as an argument, as well as an array of filenames or STDIN.

The -E parameter tells grep to use extended regular expressions, which offer more features than regular POSIX regular expressions. Two other useful parameters are -i and -v. The -i parameter tells grep to ignore case, and the -v parameter prints lines that don't match the expression.

The grep command will print lines that match STDOUT.

Using the grep Examples in This Book

You can type the GNU grep examples in this book as commands, as shown in the examples. Each of the examples uses single quotes (') to wrap the expression. This is because the shell that was used when the examples were tested—the Bash shell—doesn't interpret anything that's found within single quotes. This is a plus because many of the metacharacters in regular expressions are also special characters in most shells.

Using Expressions with sed

You can use the GNU sed command to make replacements in files or STDOUT. To use the sed command to make replacements, use 's///' as an argument to sed with the search and replacement strings in the operator, like so:

```
$ sed 's/moo/oink/' myfile
```

This prints the lines in myfile, with moo replaced with oink.

Using the sed Examples in This Book

You can type the sed examples shown in the recipes into a Unix or Linux Bash shell. The expressions are wrapped in single quotes because the shell won't attempt to translate some of the metacharacters that also have special meaning to the shell.

I tested all the sed examples in this book on Red Hat Enterprise Linux 3 using the Bash shell.

Other Examples

Throughout this book, you'll see some other examples that don't fit into the previous categories—for example, using the find command. The find command can accept a regular expression as an argument for finding files.

You can use these examples, where given, by simply typing the example into a shell. I tested all the examples of commands in this book on Red Hat Enterprise Linux 3 using the Bash shell.

## CHAPTER 1

Words and Text

This chapter includes recipes for performing some basic tasks of regular expressions, such as finding and replacing words and certain special characters such as tabs and high-ASCII characters.

Although this book isn't organized in levels of difficulty, this chapter includes many basic concepts that will make the rest of the book easier to follow. You won't have to go through this chapter to understand later ones, but it may help if you're new to regular expressions to make sure all the recipes in this chapter are easy to understand.

1-1. Finding Blank Lines

You can use this recipe for identifying blank lines in a file. Blank lines can contain spaces or tabs, or they can contain a combination of spaces and tabs. Variations on these expressions can be useful for stripping blank lines from a file.

Perl

```
#!/usr/bin/perl -w
use strict;

open( FILE, $ARGV[0] ) || die "Cannot open file!";

my $i = 0;

while ( <FILE> )
{
    $i++;
    next unless /^\s*$/;
    print "Found blank line at line $i\n";
}

close( FILE );
```

How It Works

The previous \s sequence represents a character class. A character class can match an entire category of characters, which \s does here even though it's a category that contains only tabs and spaces. Other character classes match far more examples, such as \d, which matches digits in most regular expression flavors. Character classes are shorthand ways of describing sets of characters.

Here's the expression broken down into parts:

^   starts the beginning of the line, followed by . . .

\s   any whitespace character (a tab or space) . . .

*   zero or more times, followed by . . .

$ the end of the line.

Shell Scripting

```
# grep '^[[:space:]]*$' filename
```

How It Works

The whitespace character class in grep is [[:space:]]. The grep expression, which is a Portable Operating System Interface (POSIX) expression, breaks down into the following:

^	at the beginning of the line, followed by . . .
[[:space:]]	any whitespace character (a tab or space) . . .
*	more than one time, but not required, followed by . . .
$	the end of the line.

Vim

```
/^\s*$
```

How It Works

To see how the Vim expression breaks down, refer to "How It Works" under the Perl example.

Variations

You can alter the grep recipe by adding the -v parameter to grep, which tells grep to print the lines that don't match the expression. The Perl and vi recipes have the advantage of containing a different character class that means "nonwhitespace." That character class is \S. Changing the expression in the Perl recipe to ^\S*$ will have the opposite effect as ^\s*$.

1-2. Finding Words

You can use this recipe for finding single words in a block of text. The expression will find only complete words surrounded by spaces.

Perl

```
#!/usr/bin/perl -w
use strict;

open( FILE, $ARGV[0] ) || die "Cannot open file!";

my $i = 0;

while ( <FILE> )
{
    $i++;
    next unless /\bword\b/;
    print "Found word at line $i\n";
}

close( FILE );
```

How It Works

A special character class in Perl, \b, allows you to easily search for whole words. This is an advantage because without doing a whole bunch of extra work you can make sure that a search for word, for example, doesn't yield unexpected matches such as sword.

You can easily break the regular expression shown here into the following:

\b   a word boundary (a space or beginning of a line, or punctuation) . . .

w   a *w* followed by . . .

o   an *o*, followed by . . .

r   an *r*, then . . .

d   a *d*, and finally . . .

\b   a word boundary at the end of the word.

PHP

```
<html>
<head><title>1-2 Finding words</title></head>
<body>
<form action="recipe1-2.php" method="post">
```

```
<input type="text" name="str"
        value="<?php print $_POST['str'];?>" /><br />
<input type="submit" value="Find word" /><br /><br />
<?php
if ( $_SERVER['REQUEST_METHOD'] == "POST" )
{
    $str = $_POST['str'];
    if ( preg_match( "/\bword\b/", $str ) )
    {
        print "<b>Heh heh.  You said 'word'</b>";
    }
    else
    {
        print "<b>Nope.  Didn't find it.</b>";
    }
}
?>
</form>
</body>
</html>
```

How It Works

See "How It Works" under the Perl example for a walk-through of this expression.

Python

```
import re
r = re.compile( r'\bword\b', re.M )
if r.search( open( 'sample.txt' ).read( ) ) :
    print "I finally found what I'm looking for.",
else:
    print "\"word\"s not here, man.",
```

How It Works

Refer to "How It Works" under the Perl example to see how this expression breaks down.

Shell Scripting

```
# grep '\<word\>' filename
```

How It Works

The word boundary character class \b found in Perl-Compatible Regular Expressions (PCREs) doesn't exist in extended POSIX expressions. Instead, you can use the character class \< to refer to the left word boundary and the character class \> to refer to the word boundary at the end of the word. For example:

\<	a word boundary at the beginning of the word . . .
w	a *w* followed by . . .
o	an *o*, followed by . . .
r	an *r*, then. . .
d	a *d*, and finally . . .
\>	a word boundary at the end of the word.

Vim

```
/\<word\>
```

How It Works

See "How It Works" under the shell scripting example for an explanation of this expression.

1-3. Finding Multiple Words with One Search

You can use this recipe for finding more than one word in a block of text. This recipe assumes both words are whole words surrounded by whitespace.

Perl

```
#!/usr/bin/perl -w
use strict;

open( FILE, $ARGV[0] ) || die "Cannot open file!";

my $i = 0;

while ( <FILE> )
{
    $i++;
    next unless /\s+((moo)|(oink))\s+/;
    print "Found farm animal sound at line $i\n";
}

close( FILE );
```

How It Works

Starting outside working in, this expression searches for something that's surrounded by whitespace. For example:

\s	whitespace . . .
+	found one or more times . . .
(. . .)	followed by *something* . . .
\s	followed by whitespace . . .
+	that occurs one or more times.

The something here is another expression, (moo)|(oink). This expression is as follows:

(	a group that contains . . .
m	an *m*, followed by . . .
o	an *o*, then . . .
o	an *o* . . .
)	the end of the group . . .
|	or . . .

(a group that contains . . .

o   an *o*, followed by . . .

i   an *i*, then . . .

n   an *n*, followed by . . .

k   a *k* . . .

)   the end of a group.

PHP

```
<html>
<head><title>1-3 Finding multiple words with one search</title></head>
<body>
<form action="recipe1-3.php" method="post">
<input type="text" name="str"
    value="<?php print $_POST['str'];?>" /><br />
<input type="submit" value="Find words" /><br /><br />
<?php
if ( $_SERVER['REQUEST_METHOD'] == "POST" )
{
    $str = $_POST['str'];
    if ( preg_match( "/\s+((moo)|(oink))\s+/", $str ) )
    {
        print "<b>Found match:  '" . $str . "'</b><br/>";
    }
    else
    {
        print "<b>Did NOT find match: '" . $str . "'</b><br/>";
    }
}
?>
</form>
</body>
</html>
```

How It Works

See "How It Works" under the Perl example in this recipe.

Python

```
import re
r = re.compile( r'\s+((moo)|(oink))\s+', re.M )
if r.search( open( 'sample.txt' ).read( ) ):
```

```
    print "I spy a cow or pig.",
else:
    print "Ah, there's no cow or pig here.",
```

How It Works

See "How It Works" under the Perl example.

Shell Scripting

```
$ grep '[[:space:]]\+\(\(oink\)\|\(moo\)\)[[:space:]]\+' filename
```

How It Works

The POSIX expression uses the [[:space:]] character class to identify whitespace in the expression. Starting from the outside in, the expression is as follows:

[[:space:]]	whitespace . . .
\+	found one or more times . . .
\(...\)	a group that contains something . . .
[[:space:]]	whitespace . . .
\+	found one or more times.

The something here is the expression \(oink\)\|\(moo\). This expression joins two groups of characters found inside \(and \) with the or operator \| to say, "The group of characters *o*, *i*, *n*, and *k* or the group of characters containing *m*, *o*, and *o*."

Vim

```
/\s\+\(\(oink\)\|\(moo\)\)\s\+
```

How It Works

See "How It Works" under the Perl example. Remember to escape the characters +, (,), and |.

1-4. Finding Variations on Words (John, Jon, Jonathan)

You can use this recipe for finding variations on a word with one search. This particular recipe searches for the strings Jon Doe, John Doe, or Jonathan Doe.

Perl

```
#!/usr/bin/perl -w
use strict;

my $mystr = $ARGV[0] || die "You must supply a parameter!\n";
if ( $mystr =~ /Joh?n(athan)? Doe/)
{
    print "Hello!  I've been looking for you!\n"
}
```

How It Works

This expression works by finding the common and optional parts of a word and searching based on them. John, Jon, and Jonathan are all similar. They start with *Jo* and have an *n* in them. The rest is the *h* in John or the *athan* ending in Jonathan. For example:

J	followed by . . .
o	then . . .
h	that is . . .
?	optional, followed by . . .
n	followed by . . .
(...)	a group of characters . . .
?	that may appear once, but isn't required, followed by . . .
<space>	a space, followed by . . .
D	then . . .
o	and finally . . .
e	at the end.

This group of characters is athan, which will let the expression match Jonathan. It may or may not appear as a whole part, so that's why it's grouped with parentheses and followed by ?.

PHP

```
<html>
<head><title>1-4 Finding variations on words (John, Jon, Jonathan)</title></head>
<body>
<form action="recipe1-4.php" method="post">
<input type="text" name="str"
    value="<?php print $_POST['str'];?>" /><br />
<input type="submit" value="Where is John" /><br /><br />
<?php
if ( $_SERVER['REQUEST_METHOD'] == "POST" )
{
    $str = $_POST['str'];
    if ( preg_match( "/Joh?n(athan)? Doe/", $str ) )
    {
        print "<b>Found him:  '" . $str . "'</b><br/>";
    } else {
        print "<b>Nothing:   '" . $str . "'</b><br/>";
    }
}
?>
</form>
</body>
</html>
```

How It Works

See "How It Works" under the Perl example for a detailed explanation of this expression.

Python

```
#!/usr/bin/python
import re;
import sys;

nargs = len(sys.argv);

if nargs > 1:
    mystr = sys.argv[1];

    r = re.compile(r'Joh?n(athan)? Doe', re.M)
    if r.search(mystr):
        print 'Here\'s Johnny!';
    else:
        print 'Who?';

else:
    print 'I came here for an argument!';
```

How It Works

See "How It Works" under the Perl example for a breakdown of this recipe.

Shell Scripting

```
$ grep 'Joh\?n\(athan\)\? Doe' filename
```

How It Works

See "How It Works" under the Perl example, and remember to escape the characters ?, (, and).

Vim

```
/Joh\?n\(athan\)\? Doe
```

How It Works

See "How It Works" under the Perl expression. Remember to escape the characters ?, (, and); otherwise they will be taken literally instead of having their special meanings.

Variations

One variation on this recipe is using instead an expression such as that found in recipe 1-3, like ((Jon)|(John)|(Jonathan)) Doe. Depending on the skills of your peers, this may be easy to use because it can be easier to read by someone else. Another variation on this is ((Jon(athan)?)|(John)) Doe. Writing an elegant and fast regular expression is nice, but in these days processor cycles are often cheaper than labor. Make sure whatever path you choose will be the easiest to maintain by the people in your organization.

1-5. Finding Similar Words (Bat, Cat, Mat)

Slightly different from the previous recipe, this recipe focuses on using a character class to match a single letter and the word boundary character class.

Perl

```
#!/usr/bin/perl -w
use strict;

my $mystr = $ARGV[0] || die "You must supply a parameter!\n";
if ($mystr =~ /\b[bcm]at\b/)
{
    print "Found a word rhyming with hat\n";
}
else
{
    print "That's a negatory, big buddy.\n";
}
```

How It Works

The key to the expressions in these recipes finding whole words, even those that have no spaces around them and are on lines all by themselves, is the \b character class, which specifies a word boundary. A word boundary can be any whitespace that sets a word apart from others and can also include the beginning of a line and then end of a line. The other character class that's in this expression is [bcm], which matches a single character that can be one of b, c, or m. So you can break the entire expression down like this:

\b	is a word boundary, followed by . . .
[bcm]	one of *b*, *c*, or *m*, followed by . . .
a	then . . .
t	and finally . . .
\b	a word boundary.

PHP

```
<html>
<head><title>1-5 Finding similar words (bat, cat, mat)</title></head>
<body>
<form action="recipe1-5.php" method="post">
<input type="text" name="value" value="<? print $_POST['value']; ?>"/><br/>
<input type="submit" value="Submit" /><br/><br/>
<?php
```

```
if ( $_SERVER[REQUEST_METHOD] == "POST" )
{
    $mystr = $_POST['value'];
    if ( preg_match( '/\b[bcm]at\b/', $mystr ) )
    {
        echo "Yes!<br/>";
    }
    else
    {
        echo "Uh, no.<br/>";
    }
}
?>
</form>
</body>
</html>
```

How It Works

Since this PHP example uses preg_match(), which uses PCRE, refer to "How It Works" under the Perl example to see this expression broken down.

Python

```
#!/usr/bin/python
import re;
import sys;

nargs = len(sys.argv);

if nargs > 1:
    mystr = sys.argv[1];

    r = re.compile(r'\b[bcm]at\b', re.M)
    if r.search(mystr):
        print 'I spy a bat, a cat, or a mat',
    else:
        print 'I don\'t spy nuttin\', honey',

else:
    print 'Come again?',
```

How It Works

Refer to "How It Works" under the Perl example to see how this expression breaks down into parts.

Shell Scripting

```
$ grep '\<[cbm]at\>' filename
```

How It Works

I explain this expression under "How It Works" in the Perl example, with the exception of the different word boundary. The PCRE word boundary character class \b is replaced with \< and \>.

Vim

```
/\<[cbm]at\>
```

How It Works

See "How It Works" under the shell scripting example.

Variations

A few variations on this expression exist, the most common of which is to use grouping and the or operator | instead of a character class to specify *b*, *c*, or *m*, as in \b(b|c|m)at\b.

1-6. Replacing Words

This recipe focuses on replacing complete words. It takes advantage of word anchors, which allow you to easily make sure you get an entire match.

Perl

```perl
#!/usr/bin/perl -w
use strict;

my $mystr = $ARGV[0] || die "You must supply a parameter!\n";
$mystr =~ s/\bfrick\b/frack/g;
print $mystr . "\n";
```

How It Works

This recipe has two expressions in it—the search expression and the replacement expression. Some extra characters in this expression make sure the match works on a whole word and not on a partial word. The word *frickster* will be left alone, for instance. Let's break down the search recipe:

\b	is a word boundary . . .
f	followed by . . .
r	then . . .
i	followed by . . .
c	followed by . . .
k	and finally . . .
\b	a word boundary.

Spelling out the word previously may seem a little redundant, but it really helps to distinguish a word from a sequence of characters that resembles a word. This is important to remember so you don't end up with matches and substitutions you aren't expecting.

PHP

```php
<html>
<head><title>1-6 Replacing words</title></head>
<body>
<form action="recipe1-6.php" method="post">
<input type="text" name="value" value="<? print $_POST['value']; ?>" /><br />
<input type="submit" value="Replace word" /><br /><br />
<?php
if ( $_SERVER['REQUEST_METHOD'] == "POST" )
```

```
{
    $str = $_POST['value'];
    $newstr = preg_replace( "/\bfrick\b/", "frack", $str );
    print "<b>$newstr</b><br/>";
}
?>
</form>
</body>
</html>
```

How It Works

Refer to "How It Works" under the Perl example to see this search expression broken down.

Shell Scripting

```
$ sed 's/\<frick\>/frack/g' filename
```

How It Works

POSIX regular expressions support \< as a beginning word boundary and \> as a word boundary for the end of a word. Other than those differences, this expression is the same as the one explained in "How It Works" under the Perl example in this recipe.

Vim

```
:%s/\<frick\>/frack/g
```

How It Works

See "How It Works" under the shell scripting example for an explanation of this expression.

1-7. Replacing Everything Between Two Delimiters

This recipe replaces everything inside double quotes with a different string—in this case three asterisks. You can replace the double-quote delimiter with a different character to build expressions that will replace anything inside delimiters with another string.

Perl

```
#!/usr/bin/perl -w
use strict;

my $mystr = $ARGV[0] || die "You must supply a parameter!\n";
$mystr =~ s/\"[^\"]*\"/"***"/g;
print $mystr . "\n";
```

How It Works

This recipe shows off a simple version of the recipes later in Chapter 3. The expression is saying the following:

\"	is a quote, followed by . . .
[	a character class . . .
^	that isn't . . .
\"	another quote . . .
]	the end of the character class . . .
*	zero or more times . . .
\"	another quote appears.

Why not just use \".*\" and be done with it, you say? Well, that will work. Somewhat. The problem is that a quote (") is matched by . (which matches anything). Say you have a string such as this:

```
my "string" is "water absorbent"
```

then you'll end up with this:

```
my "***"
```

PHP

```
<html>
<head><title>1-7 Replacing everything between two delimiters</title></head>
<body>
<form action="recipe1-7.php" method="post">
```

```
<input type="text" name="value" value="<? print $_POST['value']; ?>"/><br/>
<input type="submit" value="Submit" /><br/><br/>
<?php
if ( $_SERVER['REQUEST_METHOD'] == "POST" )
{
    $mystr = $_POST['value'];
    $mynewstr = ( ereg_replace( '"[^"]*"', '"***"', $mystr ) );
    print "<b>$mynewstr</b>";
}
?>
</form>
</body>
</html>
```

How It Works

Although this PHP example uses ereg_replace, which is POSIX and not PCRE, the expression is the same as the one explained in "How It Works" under the Perl example in this recipe.

One difference exists: the double quotes aren't escaped in this PHP example. The string is wrapped in single quotes, so you don't need to escape them. Quotes don't need to be escaped for regular expressions—they need to be escaped depending on the context in which they're used.

Shell Scripting

```
$ sed 's/\"[^\"]*\"/"***"/g' filename
```

How It Works

See "How It Works" under the Perl example in this recipe.

Vim

```
:%s/\"[^\"]*\"/"***"/g
```

How It Works

See "How It Works" under the Perl example in this recipe.

Variations

This recipe has plenty of room for getting fancy, depending on the flavor of regular expression you're using. Some, such as Perl, allow you to modify expressions as they're back referenced. The \U metacharacter, for instance, turns the back reference to uppercase. Here's an expression that will turn everything inside parentheses to uppercase using Perl: s/\(([^\)]*)\)/(\U$1)/g.

1-8. Replacing Tab Characters

This recipe is for replacing tab characters in a string with a different character. In this recipe, I use a pipe (|) to replace the tab.

Perl

```perl
#!/usr/bin/perl -w
use strict;

my $mystr = $ARGV[0] || die "You must supply a parameter!\n";

$mystr =~ s/\t/|/g;

print $mystr . "\n";
```

How It Works

Breaking the recipe down yields simply the following:

\t   is a tab, replaced by . . .

| a pipe character.

PHP

```php
<html>
<head><title>1-8 Replacing tab characters</title></head>
<body>
<form action="recipe1-8.php" method="post">
<input type="submit" value="Submit" /><br/><br/>
<?php
if ( $_SERVER['REQUEST_METHOD'] == "POST" )
{

    $myfile = @fopen( "recipe1-8.txt", "r" )
        or die ("Cannot open file $myfile");

    while ( $line = @fgets( $myfile, 1024 ) )
    {
        $mynewstr = ereg_replace( "\t", "|", $line);
        echo "$mynewstr<br/>";
    }
    fclose($myfile);
}
?>
```

```
</form>
</body>
</html>
```

How It Works

See "How It Works" under the Perl example in this recipe. The POSIX expression, shown here, supports the same character class for tab characters as the PCRE expressions.

Python

```
#!/usr/bin/python
import re;
import sys;

nargs = len(sys.argv);

if nargs > 1:
    mystr = sys.argv[1]
    r = re.compile(r'\t', re.M)

    returnstr = r.sub( '|', open( mystr ).read( ) );

    print returnstr,

else:
    print 'Come again?',
```

How It Works

See "How It Works" under the Perl example in this recipe for a description of this expression.

Shell Scripting

```
$ sed 's/\t/\|/g' filename
```

How It Works

You'll find this sed expression here broken down in "How It Works" under the Perl expression.

Vim

`:%s/\t/|/g`

How It Works

See "How It Works" under the Perl example for an explanation of the expression shown here. The g option will tell the Vim editor to replace all occurrences found on the line.

Variations

Since this is such a simple recipe, it has an extensive number of variations. You could replace the character class representing a tab with other character classes, especially the \s character class in Perl. The Perl variation s/\s/,/g would replace each instance of whitespace with a comma.

One variation on the previous recipe is to use a qualifier after the character class to replace more than one instance of a tab at once. For instance, if you want to replace two tabs with four spaces, you could use something such as s/\t{2}/   /g in the Perl recipe.

1-9. Testing Complexity of Passwords

This recipe tests a string to make sure it has a combination of letters and numbers in the string. This recipe heavily uses look-arounds, which aren't supported by every flavor of regular expressions. For instance, the POSIX regular expressions in PHP don't support them, so use PCRE in PHP (preg_match) to accomplish this task.

Perl

```perl
#!/usr/bin/perl -w
use strict;

my $mystr = $ARGV[0] || die "You must supply a parameter!\n";

if ( $mystr =~ /^(?=.*[A-Z])(?=.*[a-z])(?=.*[0-9]).{7,15}$/ )
{
    print "Good password!\n";
}
else
{
    print "Dude!  That's way too easy.\n";
}
```

How It Works

The look-arounds in the expression make it seem more complicated than it really is. At the heart of the expression, without the look-arounds, is the following:

^	at the beginning of the line, followed by . . .
.	any character
{7,15}	found anywhere 7 to 15 times, followed by . . .
$	the end of the line.

Now let's add the look-arounds, which are grouped by the expressions (?= and). Three of them exist in this expression: (?=.*[A-Z]), (?=.*[a-z]), and (?=.*[0-9]). These look-arounds say, "This expression must appear somewhere to the right." In this case, that's to the right of ^, which is the line anchor that anchors the beginning of the line. The first look-ahead matches anything followed by a capital letter ([A-Z]), the second matches anything followed by a lowercase letter ([a-z]), and the third matches anything followed by a number ([0-9]).

PHP

```
<html>
<head><title>1-9 Testing complexity of passwords</title></head>
<body>
<form action="recipe1-9.php" method="post">
<input type="text" name="str"
    value="<?php print htmlspecialchars($_POST['str']);?>" /><br />
<input type="submit" value="Test password" /><br /><br />
<?php
if ( $_SERVER['REQUEST_METHOD'] == "POST" )
{
    $str = $_POST['str'];
    if ( preg_match( "/^(?=.*[A-Z])(?=.*[a-z])(?=.*[0-9]).{7,15}$/", $str ) )
    {
        print "<b>Good password!:  '" .
            htmlspecialchars($str) . "'</b><br/>";
    } else {
        print "<b>That's not good enough:  '" .
            htmlspecialchars($str) . "'</b><br/>";
    }
}
?>
</form>
</body>
</html>
```

How It Works

See "How It Works" under the Perl example for an explanation of this expression.

Vim

`/^\(.*[A-Z]\)\@=\(.*[a-z]\)\@=\(.*[0-9]\)\@=.\{7,15\}$`

How It Works

Vim supports look-arounds, but their syntax is so different from those in Perl that it's worth explaining the first group here as an example.

^	at the beginning of the line . . .
\(	a group that contains . . .
.	any character . . .
*	found zero or more times, followed by . . .
[	a character class that contains . . .
A-Z	A through Z . . .
]	the end of the character class . . .
\)	the end of the group . . .
\@=	the preceding expression is a look-ahead . . .
. . .	and so on.

Variations

This one has many variations, but probably the most notable is to make the expression more complicated by adding a fourth look-ahead group that matches punctuation characters, such as `(?=.*[!@#$%^&*()])`.

Another variation is to use a different character class for the number, such as \d if the flavor of regular expressions you're using supports it.

1-10. Finding Repeated Words

You can use this recipe to find words that appear more than one time in sequence, such as *the the*.

Perl

```
#!/usr/bin/perl -w
use strict;

my $mystr = $ARGV[0] || die "You must supply a parameter!\n";

if ( $mystr =~ /\b(\w+)\s\1\b/ )
{
    print "I think I'm seeing double.\n";
}
else
{
    print "Looks okay to me.\n";
}
```

How It Works

The most important aspect of this regular expression is the back reference, which is \1 in all the previous recipes. The back reference is just a way of saying "whatever you found in the first group." The parentheses in the expression define the group. Here's a breakdown of the expression:

\b	is a word boundary, followed by . . .
(...)	a group (explained next), then . . .
\s	a space . . .
+	one or more times, then . . .
\1	whatever was found in the group, and lastly . . .
\b	a word boundary.

The group is simply (\w+), which is as follows:

\w	is a word character . . .
+	found one or more times.

This will match a word. The expression begins and ends with a word boundary anchor. This is to prevent the expression from matching a string such as quarterback backrub. If the word boundary anchors are removed, the expression will stop matching whole words.

Shell Scripting

```
$ grep -E '\<([[:alpha:]]+)[[:space:]]+\1\>' filename
```

How It Works

The breakdown of the `grep` recipe is similar to the Perl recipe.

`\<`	is a word boundary, followed by . . .
`(...)`	a group (explained next), then . . .
`[[:space:]]`	a space . . .
`+`	one or more times, then . . .
`\1`	whatever was found in the group, and lastly . . .
`\>`	a word boundary.

The group in the parentheses is `[[:alpha:]]+`, which can be broken down into the following:

`[[:alpha:]]`	an alphabetical character . . .
`+`	found one or more times.

Vim

```
/\<\(\w\+\)\s\+\1\>
```

How It Works

See "How It Works" under the Perl example in this recipe.

Variations

This recipe has a few variations. The first is to expand the character classes into longer but equal expressions, such as `[ \t\r\f\n\v]` instead of `\s` for the character class that represents whitespace. Another variation is to use `[A-z]` or `[A-Za-z]` for the `\w` character class.

1-11. Searching for Repeated Words Across Multiple Lines

Similar to recipe 1-10, this recipe allows you to search for repeated words that occur on more than one line. For example:

```
word
word
```

Perl

```perl
#!/usr/bin/perl -w
use strict;

my $mystr = "word\nword";

print $mystr;

if ( $mystr =~ /\b(\w+)[\s\n]\1\b/m )
{
    print "I think I'm seeing double.\n";
}
else
{
    print "Looks okay to me.\n";
}
```

How It Works

The expression is the same as that in recipe 1-10, with the exception of \n being added next to \s.

The "magic" part of this expression is the m option added to the search operator that allows Perl to search through multiple lines.

Python

```python
#!/usr/bin/python
import re;
import sys;

nargs = len(sys.argv);

if nargs > 1:
    mystr = sys.argv[1];

    r = re.compile(r'\b(\w+)\s+\1\b', re.M )
```

```
    if r.match( open( mystr ).read( ) ) :
        print "Found double words",
    else:
        print "No match here.",

else:
    print 'I came here for an argument.',
```

How It Works

The expression here is the same as the expression in recipe 1-10, but the previous re.M option allows Python to match across lines.

1-12. Searching for Lines Beginning with a Word

This recipe allows you to find whole words at the beginning of a line.

Perl

```
#!/usr/bin/perl -w
use strict;

my $mystr = $ARGV[0] || die "You must supply a parameter!\n";

if ( $mystr =~ /^Word\b/ )
{
    print "In the beginning was the Word.\n";
}
else
{
    print "Nope.  Not here.\n";
}
```

How It Works

The key to this expression is the line anchor metacharacter ^. You can break the expression down like this:

^	at the start of the line, followed immediately by . . .
W	then . . .
o	followed by . . .
r	then . . .
d	and lastly . . .
\b	a word boundary.

The \b character class is an anchor like the ^ line anchor. However, \b is a word anchor, and the ^ metacharacter is a line anchor.

PHP

```
<html>
<head><title>1-12 Searching for lines beginning with a word</title></head>
<body>
<form action="recipe1-12.php" method="post">
<input type="text" name="str"
    value="<?php print $_POST['str'];?>" /><br />
<input type="submit" value="Find lines" /><br /><br />
```

```php
<?php
if ( $_SERVER['REQUEST_METHOD'] == "POST" )
{
    $str = $_POST['str'];
    if ( preg_match( "/^Word\b/", $str ) )
    {
        print "<b>Found a match!:  '" . $str . "'</b><br/>";
    } else {
        print "<b>Didn't find it:  '" . $str . "'</b><br/>";
    }
}
?>
</form>
</body>
</html>
```

How It Works

See "How It Works" under the Perl example for this recipe.

Shell Scripting

```
$ grep "^Word\>" filename
```

How It Works

The \b character class used in the Perl recipe isn't supported in POSIX regular expressions like shown in the grep example previously. Instead, use \> as a word boundary to the right of the word. (\< is used as the word boundary on the left of the word.) This character class is nice to use because it takes into account characters other than spaces, such as the end of the line.

Vim

```
/^Word\>
```

How It Works

See "How It Works" under the shell scripting example.

Variations

You can perform a few tweaks to these recipes to take into account some differences, such as adding a space between the beginning of the line and the start of the word. To specify an optional space or more, use \s* in the Perl recipe and [[:space:]]* in the grep recipe. The Perl result is ^\s*Word\b, and the grep variation is ^[[:space:]]*Word\>.

1-13. Searching for Lines Ending with a Word

This recipe finds full words at the end of a line. For the purposes of this example, that word is *word*.

Perl

```
#!/usr/bin/perl -w
use strict;

my $mystr = $ARGV[0] || die "You must supply a parameter!\n";
if ( $mystr =~ /\bword$/ )
{
    print "The line ends in foo.\n";
}
else
{
    print "I see no line ending in foo.\n";
}
```

How It Works

The key to this expression is the use of character classes. Two of them are used, one to define the end of the line and one to define a word boundary, so you get only whole words when using the expression. You can break down the Perl expression like this:

\b	is a word boundary, such as a space, tab, and so on, followed by . . .
f	then . . .
o	then another . . .
o	and lastly . . .
$	the end of the line.

The line anchor $ is like the line anchor ^ because both of them are supported in nearly every flavor of regular expression. The "Syntax Overview" section at the beginning of this book highlights the different character classes supported in the various sections of regular expressions.

PHP

```
<html>
<head><title>1-13 Searching for lines ending with a word</title></head>
<body>
<form action="recipe1-13.php" method="post">
<input type="text" name="str"
    value="<?php print $_POST['str'];?>" /><br />
```

```
<input type="submit" value="Search for lines" /><br /><br />
<?php
if ( $_SERVER['REQUEST_METHOD'] == "POST" )
{
    $str = $_POST['str'];
    if ( preg_match( "/\bword$/", $str ) )
    {
        print "<b>Found a match!:  '" . $str . "'</b><br/>";
    } else {
        print "<b>Didn't find it:  '" . $str . "'</b><br/>";
    }
}
?>
</form>
</body>
</html>
```

How It Works

See "How It Works" under the Perl example.

Shell Scripting

```
$ grep '\<word$' filename
```

How It Works

The word boundary character class in POSIX expressions is \< for the beginning of the word. The expression becomes as follows:

\<   is the beginning word boundary . . .

. . .   a word . . .

$ the end of the line.

In the previous example, the word is *foo*.

Vim

`/\<word$`

How It Works

See "How It Works" under the shell scripting example in this recipe for an explanation of this expression.

Variations

You may be interested in matching lines where the word is the last word on the line, which means spaces may appear between the end of the word and the end of the line. To modify the expression to match lines with possible spaces, use the character class that matches spaces with the * qualifier, which matches none or many. The Perl expression variation looks like this: `\bfoo\s*$`. The POSIX regular expression, used by grep, looks like this: `\<foo[[:space:]]*$`.

1-14. Capitalizing the First Letter of a Word

This expression demonstrates the power of PCREs that provide ways to modify the strings captured and placed into the replacement expression using back references. Unfortunately, this recipe isn't available using POSIX regular expressions. This recipe will turn the following:

```
proper noun
```

into this:

```
Proper Noun
```

Perl

```
#!/usr/bin/perl -w
use strict;

open( FILE, $ARGV[0] ) || die "Cannot open file!";

while ( <FILE> )
{
    # print the filtered line
    my $line = $_;
    $line =~ s/\b([a-z])(\w+)\b/\u$1$2/g;
    print $line;
}

close( FILE );
```

How It Works

This expression needs to capture the first character of a word in one group and then capture the rest of the group in another group so the second group can be unaltered in the replacement expression. You can break down the search expression like this:

\b	is a word boundary, followed by . . .
[	a character class containing . . .
a	the letters *a* . . .
-	through . . .
z	*z* . . .
]	followed by . . .
\w	a word character . . .
+	one or more times, followed by . . .
\b	a word boundary.

In this breakdown, I didn't include the parentheses, which are used to capture pieces of text that match the expressions. The first grouping appears around the character class (`[a-z]`) and will grab the first letter of a word from *a* to *z*. The second group, (`\w+`), grabs the rest of the word up to its boundary.

The replacement expression breaks down into the following:

\u   changes the following reference to uppercase . . .

$1   whatever was found in the first group, followed by . . .

$2   whatever was found in the second group.

1-15. Filtering Spam

Although filtering spam is a broad topic, this recipe demonstrates a rudimentary spam filter that searches for a variation of a word, including l33t-speak equivalents. This easy filter will match the following:

```
spam
S P A M
s p a m
S P 4 M
SSSSS PPPPP AAAA MMMM
SSSSPPPPAAAAMMM
```

Perl

```perl
#!/usr/bin/perl -w
use strict;

my $mystr = $ARGV[0] || die "You must supply a parameter!\n";
if ( $mystr =~ /\b[Ss]+\s*[Pp]+\s*[Aa4]+\s*[Mm]*\b/ )
{
    print "They found me.  I don't know how, but they found me.\n";
}
```

How It Works

The purpose of this recipe is to match a sequence of characters that make up a word, which is a useful idea to filter e-mail subjects since spammers have given up saying things such as *Free pills!* and now go to uberexotic lengths such as *F R 3 3 P 1LLS!!!*

Let's break this expression down to see how it works:

\b	is a word boundary (a space, the beginning of a line, and so on), followed by . . .
[Ss]	a character class that matches either an *S* or an *s* . . .
+	one of more times (to catch repetition), followed by . . .
\s	a space . . .
*	any number of times, and maybe not at all, followed by . . .
[Pp]	a capital or lowercase *P* . . .
+	one or more times, followed by . . .
\s	a space . . .
*	any number of times . . .
[Aa4]	followed by an *A*, a, or 4 (to catch l33t-speak variations) . . .
+	one or more times, followed by . . .

\s	a space . . .
*	any number of times, followed by . . .
[Mm]	an uppercase or lowercase *M* . . .
\b	and at last a word boundary.

PHP

```
<html>
<head><title>1-15 Filtering spam</title></head>
<body>
<form action="recipe1-15.php" method="post">
<input type="text" name="value" value="<? print $_POST['value']; ?>"/><br/>
<input type="submit" value="Submit" /><br/><br/>
<?php
if ( $_SERVER['REQUEST_METHOD'] == "POST" )
{
    $mystr = $_POST['value'];
    if ( ereg( '[Ss]+[[:space:]]*[Pp]+[[:space:]]*[Aa4]+[[:space:]]*[Mm]*',
        $mystr ) )
    {
        print "<b>Haven't you got anything without spam?<b>";
    }
    else
    {
        print "No spam found here.";
    }
}
?>
</form>
</body>
</html>
```

How It Works

With the exception of using [[:space:]] instead of \s for a character class denoting white-space, this expression is identical to the PCRE version explained in "How It Works" under the Perl expression.

Shell Scripting

```
$ grep '\<[Ss]\+[[:space:]]*[Pp]\+[[:space:]]*[Aa4]\+[[:space:]]*[Mm]*\>' filename
```

How It Works

See "How It Works" under the PHP example. The additional modifications are the escaped plus (+) signs so that they aren't taken literally.

Vim

```
/\<[Ss]\+\s*[Pp]\+\s*[Aa4]\+\s*[Mm]*\>
```

How It Works

See "How It Works" under the Perl example, making sure to escape + to make it a qualifier and to use the \< and \> word anchors instead of \b.

Variations

As with any regular expression, more than one way exists to do this. One approach, although ultimately much more lengthy, could be as follows:

```
(Spam|SPAM|spam|SpAM)
```

This could get hairy when trying to list all the permutations of a word. Even the expression in this recipe is probably not effective against the most skillful spammers.

Instead of character classes, you could try something such as (S|s), but in most regular expression engines a character class is more efficient.

1-16. Filtering Profanity

You can use this recipe as a simple profanity filter. For the purpose of this recipe, let's pretend that *bleep*, *beep*, and *blankity* are naughty words. This recipe will show you how to replace those words with $@#! to print the original text with the profanity filtered out.

Perl

```perl
#!/usr/bin/perl -w
use strict;

open( FILE, $ARGV[0] ) || die "Cannot open file!";

while ( <FILE> )
{
    # print the filtered line
    my $line = $_;
    $line =~ s/\b(bleep|beep|blankity)\b/\$\@#!/gi;
    print $line;
}

close( FILE );
```

How It Works

For brevity, I won't break down the words into characters for this recipe. Here's the breakdown of the search expression:

\b	is a word boundary, followed by . . .
(	a group of expressions containing . . .
bleep	the word *bleep* . . .
		or . . .
beep	the word *beep* . . .
		or . . .
blankity	the word *blankity* . . .
)	followed by . . .
\b	a word boundary.

PHP

```
<html>
<head><title>1-16 Filtering profanity</title></head>
<body>
<form action="recipe1-16.php" method="post">
<input type="text" name="value" value="<? print $_POST['value']; ?>"/><br/>
<input type="submit" value="Submit" /><br/><br/>
<?php
if ( $_SERVER['REQUEST_METHOD'] == "POST" )
{
    $mystr = $_POST['value'];
    $mycleanstr = ereg_replace( '(bleep|beep|blankity)', '$@#!', $mystr );
    print "<b>$mycleanstr</b>";
}
?>
</form>
</body>
</html>
```

How It Works

This PHP example uses a POSIX expression supported by ereg_replace() instead of a PCRE expression supported by preg_replace(). For more information about the difference between the two, see the "Syntax Overview" section at the beginning of this book.

Like the expression in the Perl example, I won't break down the words into characters for this POSIX expression. Here's the breakdown of the search expression:

(	starts a group of expressions containing . . .
bleep	the word *bleep* . . .
|	or . . .
beep	the word *beep* . . .
|	or . . .
blankity	the word *blankity* . . .
)	the end of the group.

Shell Scripting

```
$ sed 's/\<\(bleep\|beep\|blankity\)/$@#!/gi' filename
```

How It Works

See "How It Works" under the PHP example in this recipe for an explanation of this expression.

Vim

```
:%s/\<\(bleep\|beep\|blankity\)/$@#!/g
```

How It Works

See "How It Works" under the PHP example in this recipe.

Variations

For a variation on this recipe, you could change the word match—you could condense it. Be careful about how much the expressions are condensed, because sometimes they can become unreadable and harder to maintain in the future.

Here's a condensed version of the three-word match:

```
b(l?eep|lankity)
```

1-17. Finding Strings in Quotes

You can use this recipe to find a set of words (a string) that matches only if the string is inside quotes.

Perl

```perl
#!/usr/bin/perl -w
use strict;

open( FILE, $ARGV[0] ) || die "Cannot open file!";

while ( <FILE> )
{
    # print the filtered line
    my $line = $_;
    if ( $line =~ /"[^"]*\bneat saying\b[^"]*"/ )
    {
        print $line;
    }
}

close( FILE );
```

How It Works

This expression makes sure that no quotes are found between the opening quote and the word. This will ensure that the expression is found in quotes.

"	is a quote, followed by . . .
[	a character class . . .
^	that isn't . . .
"	a quote . . .
]	appearing . . .
*	zero or more times, then . . .
\b	a word boundary . . .
...	then the words (omitted here), followed by . . .
\b	another word boundary, then . . .
[	a character class . . .
^	that isn't . . .
"	a quote . . .

]   the end of the character class . . .

*   appearing zero or more times . . .

"   the last double quote.

PHP

```
<html>
<head><title>1-17 Finding strings in quotes</title></head>
<body>
<form action="recipe1-17.php" method="post">
<input type="text" name="str"
    value="<?php print htmlspecialchars($_POST['str']);?>" /><br />
<input type="submit" value="Search" /><br /><br />
<?php
if ( $_SERVER['REQUEST_METHOD'] == "POST" )
{
    $str = $_POST['str'];
    if ( preg_match( "/\"[^\"]*\bneat saying\b[^\"]*\"/", $str ) )
    {
        print "<b>Found a match!:  '" . $str . "'</b><br/>";
    } else {
        print "<b>Didn't find it:  '" . $str . "'</b><br/>";
    }
}
?>
</form>
</body>
</html>
```

How It Works

See "How It Works" under the Perl example in this recipe for an explanation of the expression.

Shell Scripting

```
$ grep '\"[^\"]*\<neat saying\>[^\"]*\"' filename
```

How It Works

Two things make this expression different from the one broken down in "How It Works" under the Perl example: the \b word anchor is replaced by \< and \>, and the double quotes are escaped. Other than those two differences, you can get the gist of the expression by following along under the Perl example.

Vim

```
/\"[^\"]*\<neat saying\>[^\"]*\"
```

How It Works

See "How It Works" under the Perl example. Remember to replace \b with \< and \> and escape the double quotes when following along.

1-18. Escaping Quotes

You can use this recipe to add an escape character in front of double quotes that already aren't escaped. It's ideal for preparing strings to be wrapped in quotes, where all the existing quotes must have an escape sequence added to them. For the purposes of this recipe, the escape character is \.

Perl

```perl
#!/usr/bin/perl -w
use strict;

open( FILE, $ARGV[0] ) || die "Cannot open file!";

while ( <FILE> )
{
    # print the filtered line
    my $line = $_;
    $line =~ s/(^|(?<!\\))\"/\\\"/g;
    print $line;
}

close( FILE );
```

How It Works

The recipes in this section are a little different from each other because of the features that different flavors of regular expressions support. Most PCREs support look-arounds, which provide the ability to define what comes before and after the expression. These come in handy in situations such as this one, where the expression is saying, "Show me quotes that don't have escape characters in front of them."

It's best to start looking at this one by breaking it down into smaller expressions:

(...)   is a grouped expression, followed by . . .

\"   a double quote.

The grouped expression breaks down as follows:

^   the beginning of the line . . .

| or . . .

(?<!   the beginning of a negative look-behind . . .

\\   an escaped \ . . .

)   the end of the negative look-behind.

The negative look-behind expression is defined by (?<!. Everything between that and the closing parenthesis,), is evaluated. So the recipe (^|(?<!\\))\" will match a quote as long as it isn't preceded by a backslash (\) or is proceeded by a newline (^).

PHP

```
<html>
<head><title>1-18 Escaping quotes</title></head>
<body>
<form action="recipe1-18.php" method="post">
<input type="text" name="value"
value="<? htmlspecialchars($_POST['value']);?>" /><br/><br/>
<input type="submit" value="Submit" /><br/><br/>
<?php
if ( $_SERVER['REQUEST_METHOD'] == "POST" )
{
    $mystr = $_POST['value'];
    $mynewstr = preg_replace( '/(^|(?<!\\\))\"/', '\\\"', $mystr);
    print "<b>" . htmlspecialchars($mynewstr) . "</b>";
}
?>
</form>
</body>
</html>
```

How It Works

Refer to "How It Works" under the Perl example to see how this expression breaks down into parts.

Note The look-behind has an extra \: (?<!\\\). This is intentional. In the version of PHP I was using when I wrote this, a bug didn't allow the Perl expression to work straight from the Perl script. Adding the extra \ seemed to resolve the issue.

Vim

```
:%s/\(^\|\(\\\)\@<!\)\"/\\\"/g
```

How It Works

The Vim recipe works also by using a look-behind, but the syntax is different from a PCRE expression. Here, the grouped expression is as follows:

\(starts the group . . .

^   a line anchor . . .

\| or . . .

\(the beginning of a second group . . .

\\   an escape character . . .

\)   the end of the group . . .

\@<!   the previous expression is a negative look-behind . . .

\)   the end of the group.

1-19. Removing Escaped Sequences

This recipe removes escape characters such as \ unless they're escaped themselves. So given a string such as \slashes\\, this recipe will yield slashes\\.

Perl

```
#!/usr/bin/perl -w
use strict;

open( FILE, $ARGV[0] ) || die "Cannot open file!";

while ( <FILE> )
{
    # print the filtered line
    my $line = $_;
    $line =~ s/(?<![\\])\\(?!\\)//g;
    print $line;
}

close( FILE );
```

How It Works

Let's examine how this expression works and why it's more involved than something such as s/\\//g (which will remove every slash). You can break the Perl expression down like this:

(?<!	is a look-behind expression that *doesn't* match . . .
[\\]	a character that's a slash . . .
)	(end of the look-behind expression) followed by . . .
\\	a slash, where . . .
(?!	a look-ahead expression that *doesn't* match . . .
\\	another slash . . .
)	(end of the look-ahead expression).

PHP

```
<html>
<head><title>1-19 Removing escape characters</title></head>
<body>
<form action="recipe1-19.php" method="post">
<input type="text" name="value"
value="<? htmlspecialchars($_POST['value']); ?>" /><br/><br/>
```

```
<input type="submit" value="Submit" /><br/><br/>
<?php
if ( $_SERVER['REQUEST_METHOD'] == "POST" )
{
        $mystr = $_POST['value'];
        $mynewstr = preg_replace( '/(?<![\\\])\\\(?!\\\)/', '', $mystr);
        print "<b>" . htmlspecialchars($mynewstr) . "</b>";
}
?>
</form>
</body>
</html>
```

How It Works

See "How It Works" under the Perl example for an explanation of this expression.

1-20. Adding Semicolons at the End of a Line

This recipe will add a semicolon to the end of each line. This recipe can come in handy to turn lines of regular text to lines of code. Variations on this recipe allow you to add a comma to the end of a line. Since the POSIX and Perl-compatible versions of this recipe are identical, I'll show only the Perl recipe here.

Perl

```
#!/usr/bin/perl -w
use strict;

open( FILE, $ARGV[0] ) || die "Cannot open file!";

while ( <FILE> )
{
    # print the filtered line
    my $line = $_;
    $line =~ s/$/;/;
    print $line;
}

close( FILE );
```

How It Works

This recipe is fairly straightforward—it simply demonstrates the use of the $ metacharacter that matches the end of a line. You can break the match portion of the recipe down like this:

$ marks the end of the line.

The replacement section is simply as follows:

;   is a semicolon.

Variations

This expression has quite a few useful variations. Note that s/$/;/ isn't particularly an "intelligent" expression. It doesn't perform tasks such as check to see if the line already ends in ;. You can easily add this by using the negation operator ^ in the expression. The result is s/[^;]$/;/. Why not s/^;$/;/? Although it looks really similar, it's saying something different. The ^ character is the negation character only when it's inside a character class. Outside a character class, ^ means "the beginning of the line."

Other variations include adding something other than ; at the end of the line. You do this by just swapping out the ; character in the replacement expression with something else, such as a comma or a period.

1-21. Adding to the Beginning of a Line

Sometimes it's useful to add text at the beginning of a line. In the "real world," I've used this recipe along with recipe 1-20 to turn lines of a file into code statements. For example, you can turn the following:

```
This line
That line
```

into this:

```
string.Add( "This line" );
string.Add( "That line" );
```

In the "Variations" section at the end of this recipe, I'll show you how to do that in one expression instead of two.

Perl

```
#!/usr/bin/perl -w
use strict;

open( FILE, $ARGV[0] ) || die "Cannot open file!";

while ( <FILE> )
{
    my $line = $_;
    $line =~ s/^/line:  /;
    print $line;
}

close( FILE );
```

How It Works

Like the 1-20 recipe, this one is straightforward. It uses the ^ metacharacter, which is a line anchor. This line anchor means "the beginning of the line," so the breakdown of the search recipe is simply as follows:

^   indicates the beginning of the line.

The replacement expression is anything you want to add to the beginning of the line. For this replacement, you don't need to have anything special such as back references or grouping. The line anchor ^ doesn't even need to be in the replacement expression.

Variations

As I mentioned previously, one of the variations on this expression is the combination of the two expressions to add text to the beginning and end of the line at the same time. This has many uses—consider a list that you want to modify into lines of code or a set of lines that you want to enclose in quotes. Here, I use back references to insert everything between the beginning and the end of the line back into the replacement expression: `s/^(.*)$/list.add("$1")/`. This expression, when used on a file that contains the following:

```
apples
bananas
celery
```

will print this:

```
list.add("apples");
list.add("bananas");
list.add("celery");
```

Another variation is to use another metacharacter, such as \t, in the replacement expression. Using \t as the replacement expression will indent each line with a tab.

1-22. Replacing Smart Quotes with Straight Quotes

You can use this recipe to replace smart quotes (" and "), inserted by some word processors, with ordinary straight quotes (" and "). This recipe comes in handy when cutting and pasting from a word processor file into a code file or Hypertext Markup Language (HTML) file, where the smart quotes can sometimes cause issues.

Unfortunately, this recipe is limited to regular expression flavors that support Unicode or hex sequences. The PHP recipe, for instance, uses preg_replace instead of ereg_replace to take advantage of PCREs.

Perl

```
#!/usr/bin/perl -w
use strict;

open( FILE, $ARGV[0] ) || die "Cannot open file!";

while ( <FILE> )
{
    my $line = $_;
    $line =~ s/\x93|\x94/"/g;
    print $line;
}

close( FILE );
```

How It Works

Perl supports specifying a character by its hexadecimal value by using the \xNN character class, where NN is the character's hexadecimal value.

\x93   is a left double quote . . .

| or . . .

\x94   is a right double quote.

And the replacement expression is simply ", which is a straight double quote.

PHP

```
<html>
<head><title>1-22 Replacing smart quotes with straight quotes</title></head>
<body>
<form action="recipe1-22.php" method="post">
<input type="text" name="value" value="<? print $_POST['value']; ?>"/><br/><br/>
```

```php
<input type="submit" value="Submit" /><br/><br/>
<?php
if ( $_SERVER['REQUEST_METHOD'] == "POST" )
{
        $mystr = $_POST['value'];
        $mynewstr = preg_replace( '/\x93|\x94/', '"', $mystr );
        print "<b>$mynewstr</b>";
}
?>
</form>
</body>
</html>
```

How It Works

See "How It Works" under the Perl example in this recipe.

Variations

You can specify the smart quotes by their octal value as well as by their hex value. This can be handy because if you're on a Unix or Linux command line, you can use a utility called hexdump (which deprecates od) that will dump the contents of a file in octal, hex, or ASCII values. Use the -c option to print the file in a format from which you can grab the octal values. The octal values for the smart quotes are 222 and 223 for the right and left quotes, respectively. So you can use s/\u222|\u223/"/g to replace straight quotes as well.

1-23. Replacing Copyright Symbols

This recipe shows you how to replace a copyright symbol (©) with the sequence (c), which may be necessary for some files. Some editors automatically replace the (c) sequence with the other character, and that could lead to problems in files that are supposed to be plain ASCII text.

Perl

```perl
#!/usr/bin/perl -w
use strict;

open( FILE, $ARGV[0] ) || die "Cannot open file!";

while ( <FILE> )
{
    my $line = $_;
    $line =~ s/\x97/(c)/g;
    print $line;
}

close( FILE );
```

How It Works

The match regular expression can be broken down into the following:

\x97   is the © special character.

1-24. Replacing ™ with (TM)

This recipe takes advantage of hex escapes to replace the ™ special character with a standard (TM) sequence that can be better displayed in plain text and HTML formats. A variation on this recipe includes swapping the special character out with an HTML entity.

Perl

```
#!/usr/bin/perl -w
use strict;

open( FILE, $ARGV[0] ) || die "Cannot open file!";

while ( <FILE> )
{
    my $line = $_;
    $line =~ s/\x99/(TM)/g;
    print $line;
}

close( FILE );
```

How It Works

You can break the match regular expression down into the following:

\x99   is the ™ special character.

And that's about it—nothing else to see here.

PHP

```
<html>
<head><title>1-24 Replacing &tm; with (TM)</title></head>
<body>
<form action="recipe1-24.php" method="post">
<input type="text" name="value" value="<? print $_POST['value']; ?>"/><br/><br/>
<input type="submit" value="Submit" /><br/><br/>
<?php
if ( $_SERVER['REQUEST_METHOD'] == "POST" )
{
    $mystr = $_POST['value'];
    $mynewstr = preg_replace( '/\x99/', '(TM)', $mystr);
    print "<b>$mynewstr</b>";
}
?>
```

```
</form>
</body>
</html>
```

How It Works

See "How It Works" under the Perl example.

Variations

One useful variation on this theme is to replace the (TM) replacement expression with the HTML entity ™. You can use this entity instead of (TM) to display the symbol correctly in an HTML page.

1-25. Splitting Lines in a File

You can use this recipe to split words that are separated by commas onto separate lines. This can be useful to make lists more readable by placing each item of a list on a line all by itself. For example, a line such as this:

```
apples, bananas, celery
```

becomes the following:

```
apples,
bananas,
celery
```

Perl

```perl
#!/usr/bin/perl -w
use strict;
my $line = $ARGV[0];
$line =~ s/,\s*/,\n/g;
print $line. "\n";
```

How It Works

This recipe uses a character class and a qualifier to enhance the expression to make the results a little cleaner. Here's a breakdown of the match expression:

,	is a comma followed by . . .
\s	a space . . .
*	none or many times.

The replacement expression is simply as follows:

,	is a comma followed by . . .
\n	a newline character.

The spaces after the comma go away when the replacement is made. Each line will end with a comma. The newline character, \n, will insert a line break into the replacement string.

PHP

```php
<html>
<head><title>1-25 Splitting lines in a file</title></head>
<body>
<form action="recipe1-25.php" method="post">
<input type="text" name="value"
    value="<? print $_POST['value']; ?>" /><br/><br/>
```

```
<input type="submit" value="Submit" /><br/><br/>
<?php
if ( $_SERVER[REQUEST_METHOD] == "POST" )
{
    $mystr = $_POST['value'];
    $mynewstr = ereg_replace( ',[[:space:]]*', ',<br />', $mystr);
    print "<b>$mynewstr</b>";
}
?>
</form>
</body>
</html>
```

How It Works

See "How It Works" under the Perl example in this recipe for an explanation.

Python

```
#!/usr/bin/python
import re;
import sys;

nargs = len(sys.argv);

if nargs > 1:
    mystr = sys.argv[1];
    r = re.compile( r',\s*', re.M | re.I )
    newstr = r.sub( ',\n', open( mystr ).read( ) )
    print newstr,

else:
    print 'Filename?  Anyone?  Anyone?',
```

How It Works

See "How It Works" under the Perl example for a walk-through of this recipe.

1-26. Joining Lines in a File

You can use this recipe for combining lines in a file but splitting them with another character such as a comma. For example, a file with lines such as this:

```
one
ring
to
rule
```

becomes the following:

```
one, ring, to, rule
```

Perl

```perl
#!/usr/bin/perl -w
use strict;

open( FILE, $ARGV[0] ) || die "Cannot open file!";

while ( <FILE> )
{
    my $line = $_;
    $line =~ s/\n/, /mg;
    print $line;
}

print "\n";

close( FILE );
```

How It Works

This recipe breaks down into very few parts:

\n	is a newline, replaced by . . .
,	a comma followed by . . .
<space>	a space.

The options available to the various scripting languages and regular expression objects allow the expression to be applied over multiple lines. In Perl, that's the m modifier at the end of the expression (as in s///m).

Python

```
#!/usr/bin/python
import re;
import sys;

nargs = len(sys.argv);

if nargs > 1:
    mystr = sys.argv[1];
    r = re.compile( r'\n', re.M | re.I )
    newstr = r.sub( ', ', open( mystr ).read( ) )
    print newstr,

else:
    print 'Filename?  Anyone?  Anyone?',
```

How It Works

See "How It Works" under the Perl example. A difference exists in the implementation of the expression across multiple lines. In Python, you accomplish that by using the re.M flag when compiling the expression.

1-27. Removing Everything on a Line After a Certain Character

In this recipe, everything after # on a line is going to be removed, including the # sign. This can be useful for deleting line comments from scripts. For example, the recipe will turn this:

```
# This is a test line
Keep me #but remove me
```

into the following:

```
Keep me
```

Perl

```perl
#!/usr/bin/perl -w
use strict;

open( FILE, $ARGV[0] ) || die "Cannot open file!";

while ( <FILE> )
{
    # print the filtered line
    my $line = $_;
    $line =~ s/#.*$//g;
    print $line;
}

close( FILE );
```

How It Works

You can break the recipe like this:

#	followed by . . .
.	any character . . .
*	any number of times, until . . .
$	then end of the line.

The main concept in this expression is the use of the . wildcard, which matches any character. Using .* together is something you have to be careful with because it matches any character any number of times. Regular expressions are best when they're as specific as possible, even though they can be very generic.

Shell Scripting

```
$ sed 's/#.*$//g' filename
```

How It Works

See "How It Works" under the Perl example.

Vim

```
:%s/#.*$//g
```

How It Works

See "How It Works" under the Perl recipe if you're curious about how this expression breaks down.

CHAPTER 2

■■■

URLs and Paths

The recipes in this chapter focus on uniform resource locators (URLs) and file paths. These recipes can come in handy when you're trying to extract filenames, extensions, or hostnames.

2-1. Finding Log Files with Ranges

You can use this recipe to search a directory and locate files. These files use dates as part of their names, so the recipe uses regular expressions to find files within a certain date range. This recipe will match log-20040625.log but not log-20040630.log.

Perl

```perl
#!/usr/bin/perl -w
use strict;

opendir( CURDIR, '.' ) || die "The ship can't take much more of this, captain!\n";
my @files = readdir CURDIR;
closedir CURDIR;

foreach my $file ( @files )
{
    if ( $file =~ /log[-]200406(0[1-9]|[12][0-9])\.log/ )
    {
        print "$file\n";
    }
}
```

How It Works

This expression uses ranges, grouping, the or operator |, and escapes to identify literal characters.

log	indicates l, o, or g followed by ...
[-]	a character class that includes a slash, then ...
2004	the YYYY part of the filename, followed by ...
06	the MM part of the filename, then ...
(	the beginning of a group that includes ...
0	a '0', followed by ...
[1-9]	a character class that includes 1 through 9 ...
|	or ...
[12]	a character class that includes a 1 or a 2 followed by ...
[0-9]	a character class that includes 0 through 9 ...
)	the end of the group ...
\.	a literal ., which ...
log	ends in a log extension.

PHP

```
<html>
<head><title>2-1 Finding log files with ranges</title></head>
<body>
<form action="recipe2-1.php" method="post">
<input type="submit" value="Find my text files" /><br/><br/>
<?php
if ( $_SERVER['REQUEST_METHOD'] == "POST" )
{
    $dir = opendir( '/var/tmp' );
    while ( $file = readdir( $dir ) )
    {
        if ( preg_match( '/log[-]200406(0[1-9]|2[0-9])\.log/', $file ) )
        {
            print "Found file:  <b>$file</b><br />";
        }
    }
}
?>
</form>
</body>
</html>
```

How It Works

The previous PHP recipe uses Perl-Compatible Regular Expressions (PCREs) provided by preg_match(). To break this recipe down, take a look at the "How It Works" section under the Perl recipe. The function preg_match() will return true if a match is found.

Shell Scripting

```
$ find . -regex '\.\/log[-]200406\(0[1-9]\|[12][0-9]\)\.log'
```

or

```
$ ls -l | grep '\log[-]200406\(0[1-9]\|[12][0-9]\)\.log'
```

How It Works

The expressions in the shell recipes have additional escape characters in them because of the differences in regular expression implementations, particularly \(, \|, and \). These characters are escaped, so the shell doesn't try to interpret them.

Variations

Since this expression uses ranges to specify dates, the most common variations are ones on the ranges. The group (0[1-9]|[12][0-9]) will cover any number from 1 through 29. To get the expression to cover the 30th and 31st of the month, extend the group to something such as this: (0[1-9]|[12][0-9]|3[01]). You may wonder why you can't shorten the expression to something a lot simpler, such as ([0-3][0-9]). This expression, while much shorter and easier to read, will catch a lot of invalid numbers. It will catch 00, for instance, and also 32–39.

If you want to capture an arbitrary range such as 17–23, just slice the numbers to determine what ranges are appropriate. To capture this range you'll need 17–19 and also 20–23, so the expression is (1[7-9]|2[0-3]).

2-2. Extracting Query Strings from URLs

This recipe matches a query string in a URL. This expression assumes that includes everything after the first question mark (?) found in the string. Back references and matches print everything found after the ?. In the string `http://www.domain.com/index.aspx?param=foo`, the string `param=foo` will be extracted.

Perl

```perl
#!/usr/bin/perl -w
use strict;

my $mystr = $ARGV[0] || die "Please supply a parameter";

if ( $mystr =~ s/^[^?]*\?(.*)$/$1/ )
{
    print $mystr . "\n";
}
else
{
    print "No query string here.\n";
}
```

How It Works

You can break down the expression into the following parts:

^	the beginning of the string, followed by . . .
[^?]	a character class that matches anything that isn't a question mark . . .
*	found zero or more times, followed by . . .
\?	a question mark, escaped so it's taken literally, followed by . . .
(	a group that contains . . .
.	any character . . .
*	found zero or more times . . .
)	the end of the group . . .
$	the end of the line.

The gist of this expression is to capture everything after the first literal question mark all the way up to the end of the line. The expression `.*` is another way of saying, "Everything, including nothing." The character class at the beginning `[^?]` is important, because it matches everything that isn't a question mark. When the ^ is found inside square brackets, it's a negation character that means "not." Like many other characters, a ? inside brackets is taken literally and doesn't need to be escaped.

URLS AND PATHS

Perl uses $1 as a back reference, which holds the first group of characters captured by a pair of parentheses from left to right.

PHP

```
<html>
<head><title>2-2 Extracting query strings from URLs</title></head>
<body>
<form action="recipe2-2.php" method="post">
<input type="text" name="value" value=<? echo $_POST['value']; ?>/>< br/>
<input type="submit" value="Submit" /><br/><br/>
<?php
if ( $_SERVER[REQUEST_METHOD] == "POST" )
{
    $mystr = $_POST['value'];
    if ( ereg( '^[^?]*\?(.*)$', $mystr, $matches ) )
    {
        echo "Query string:  $matches[1]";
    }
    else
    {
        echo "Found no query string";
    }
}
?>
</form>
</body>
</html>
```

How It Works

This PHP recipe shows an example of using ereg(). Since the syntax for the Portable Operating System Interface (POSIX) version of the expression is the same as the PCRE version, you can walk through this expression under "How It Works" in the Perl example.

Shell Scripting

```
$ echo url | sed 's/^[^\?]*\?\(.*\)$/\1/'
```

How It Works

Remember that expressions in sed and grep work differently than in Perl when it comes to the characters ?, +, {, }, |, (, and). You need to escape them to turn them into special characters. (They're literal if they aren't escaped.) Hence, this pattern has a few escapes added that would otherwise be identical to its PCRE counterpart.

Vim

```
:%s/^[^\?]*\?\(.*\)$/\1/g
```

How It Works

The Vim expression requires the characters ?, (, and) to be escaped. Typing this command will replace the URL found on the current line with just the query string.

Variations

You can modify this expression to double-check for http:// at the beginning of the string to make sure it's really a URL. I didn't do that in this recipe for brevity, but it doesn't hurt to make the expression as specific as you can.

2-3. Extracting Hostnames from URLs

This recipe will grab the fully qualified hostname for a URL. From a URL such as http://host.domain.com/index.html, this expression will match host.domain.com. If a port is specified, such as http://host.domain.com:8080/index.html, it will capture host.domain.com:8080. It doesn't check to make sure the hostname looks like a valid hostname.

Perl

```
#!/usr/bin/perl -w
use strict;

my $mystr = $ARGV[0] || die "Please supply a parameter";

if ( $mystr =~ s/^https?:\/\/([^\/]+)\/?.*$/$1/ )
{
    print "The domain is '" . $mystr . "'\n";
}
else
{
    print "No hostname or anything like that in this string.\n";
}
```

How It Works

This expression uses parentheses to capture strings that can later be used in the back references. You may recognize some concepts from the previous recipe in this one.

You can break the expression down into the following parts:

^	the beginning of the string, followed by . . .
http	the letters *h*, *t*, *t*, and *p*, followed by . . .
s	an *s* . . .
?	found zero or one time, followed by . . .
:	a colon, then . . .
\/	an escaped slash, followed by . . .
\/	another escaped slash, and then . . .
(	the start of a group that includes . . .
[^\/]	a character class that's anything that isn't a / . . .
+	found one or more times . . .
)	the end of the group, up to . . .
\/	a slash . . .

?	that may appear at most one time, then . . .
.	any character . . .
*	found zero or more times, and lastly . . .
$	the end of the string.

The ? qualifier after the s makes sure that both http:// and https:// are matched in the string.

PHP

```
<html>
<head><title>2-3 Extracting hostnames from URLs</title></head>
<body>
<form action="recipe2-3.php" method="post">
<input type="text" name="value" value="<? print $_POST ['value']; ?>"/><br/>
<input type="submit" value="Submit" /><br/><br/>
<?php
if ( $_SERVER['REQUEST_METHOD'] == "POST" )
{
    $mystr = $_POST['value'];
    if ( ereg('^https?://([^/]+)/?.*$', $mystr ) )
    {
        if ( $hostname = preg_replace('/^https?:\/\/([^\/]+)\/?.*$/',
        '\1', $mystr ) );
        {
        print "Your hostname (and maybe port) is: $hostname";
        }
    }
}
?>
</form>
</body>
</html>
```

How It Works

See "How It Works" under the Perl recipe to walk through this expression.

Python

```
#!/usr/bin/python
import re;
import sys;
```

```
nargs = len(sys.argv);
if nargs > 1:
    mystr = sys.argv[1];
    r = re.compile( r'^https?:\/\/([^\/]+)\/?.*$', re.I );
    hostname = r.sub( r'\1', mystr )
    print 'Hostname is: ' + hostname ,
else:
    print 'Filename?  Anyone?  Anyone?',
```

How It Works

See "How It Works" under the Perl recipe to walk through this expression.

Shell Scripting

```
echo 'http://www.example.com/index.html' | \
    sed 's/^https\?:\/\/\([^\/]\+\)\/\?.*$/\1/'
```

How It Works

See "How It Works" under the Perl example, but remember that you need to escape (,), ?, and + with a \.

Vim

s/^https\?:\/\/\([^\/]\+\)\/\?.*$/\1

How It Works

See "How It Works" under the Perl example to walk through this expression. The only difference between this and the PCRE expression is that the ?, (,), and + characters are escaped with a \. Also, remember that back references are accessed by using \1 instead of $1.

Variations

One variation on this recipe is to attempt to slice the hostname into smaller chunks. Given http://host.domain.com, you may want to just match host instead of host.domain.com. To change this to match everything up to the ., swap out the \/ sequence with \.. The expression is http:\/\/([^\/.]*)[\.\/]?.*$.

2-4. Formatting URLs

This regular expression finds a string that starts with www somewhere in a string. If it finds www, it changes the string to start with http://. The line

```
hello, my home page is www.homepage.com
```

turns into the following line:

```
hello, my home page is http://www.homepage.com
```

Perl

```perl
#!/usr/bin/perl -w
use strict;

my $mystr = $ARGV[0] || die "Please supply a parameter";

# find strings that start with www and append http://
$mystr =~ s/\b(www\.\S+)/http:\/\//$1/g;
print $mystr . "\n";
```

How It Works

At first it may appear odd—not to mention unbalanced—that the expression starts with \b but doesn't end in \b like many of the recipes in this book do when dealing with whole words. The reason is because some of the characters that can form a word boundary are valid URL characters, and using \b at the end of the expression may cause it to not capture enough information.

This expression, when it finds something in a string that starts with www., will grab everything up to the next space or end-of-line and assume that it's the full URL. Here's the expression broken down:

\b	a word anchor, followed by . . .
(	a group containing . . .
www	the letters *w*, *w*, and *w*, then . . .
\.	a literal ., followed by . . .
\S	any nonwhitespace character . . .
+	found one or more times . . .
)	the end of the group.

PHP

```
<html>
<head><title>2-4 Formatting URLs</title></head>
<body>
<form action="recipe2-4.php" method="post">
<input type="text" name="value" value="<? print $_POST ['value']; ?>"/><br/>
<input type="submit" value="Submit" /><br/><br/>
<?php
if ( $_SERVER[REQUEST_METHOD] == "POST" )
{
    $mystr = $_POST['value'];
    if ( ereg( '(^|[[:space:]])(www\..*)([[:space:]]|$)', $mystr, $matches ))
    {
        echo "You really should write it like this:  http://$matches[2]";
    }
}
?>
</form>
</body>
</html>
```

How It Works

PHP's ereg() and ereg_replace() don't support a word boundary character in the same fashion as Perl, so the PHP expression is a little different. It uses the combination of the [[:space:]] character class, which matches tabs and spaces, with the or operator and line anchors.

You can break the expression down into the following:

(	the line starts with a group that matches either . . .
^	the beginning of the line . . .
|	or . . .
[[:space:]]	some whitespace . . .
)	and is followed by . . .
(	another group, containing . . .
www	three *w* characters, then . . .
\.	a literal period, or *dot*, then . . .
.	any character . . .

*	zero, one, or many times . . .
)	followed by . . .
(	another group that contains . . .
[[:space:]]	some whitespace . . .
|	or . . .
$	the end of the line . . .
)	the end of the group.

The PHP recipe uses back references via the $matches array to print what it found in the second group.

Shell Scripting

```
$ sed 's/\(^\|[[:space:]]\)\(www\..*\)\([[:space:]]\|\$\)/\1http:\/\/\2\3/g' filename
```

How It Works

The sed command doesn't support noncapturing parentheses, which is important to remember when using groups at the beginning and end of the expression, as shown here. In this case, just remember to reference all the groups so you construct the string how it was before.

Look at the PHP ereg() example in this recipe for more information on how this expression works.

Vim

```
:%s/\(^\|\s\)\(www\..*\)\(\s\|\$\)/\1http:\/\/\2\3/g
```

How It Works

The Vim editor supports \s as a character class but requires that (,), |, and $ be escaped.

Variations

At first, this expression may appear needlessly complex. You may say to yourself, "Self, I could use a find-and-replace dealybobber on my text editor and just replace www with http://www and be done with it." You'll probably be right 90 percent of the time. The problems will occur when www is found where you don't want to put http:// in front of it—that's why using regular expressions is handy.

One variation you could make on this recipe is to not limit the search expression to domain names that start with www. Maybe you want to look instead for something outside this realm of site and sound that ends in .com, .edu, or .info. OK, maybe you can't use regular expressions to find strings in alternate realities, but you can certainly modify them to match strings that end in .com, .edu, or .info, like so:

`(^|[[:space:]])([^[[:space:]]]+\.(com|edu|info))([[:space:]]|$)`

Finally, you could rewrite this to not use back references at all. Just replace `(^|[[:space:]])(www\.)` with `http://www\.`.

2-5. Translating Unix Paths to DOS Paths

This recipe can be useful, especially on Windows computers that have Cygwin installed on them. In a default installation, a Cygwin path may look like this: /cygdrive/c/Windows/ system32/drivers/etc/hosts. This expression will translate this path to C:\Windows\system32\ drivers\etc\hosts.

Perl

```perl
#!/usr/bin/perl -w

use strict;

my $path = $ARGV[0] || die "Whatchew talkin' 'bout, Willis?";

$path =~ s/^\/cygdrive\/([a-z])\//\U$1:\\/;
$path =~ s/\//\\/g;

print $path;

exit 0;
```

How It Works

This script delivers a one-two punch to change a Cygwin path to the proper Windows DOS counterpart. You can use the second expression as-is to change the path separator from / to \.

Here's the first expression broken down:

^	a line anchor . . .
\/	the root / . . .
cygdrive	used to identify the cygdrive directory . . .
\/	the second path separator . . .
(	a capturing group that contains . . .
[	a character class with . . .
a-z	the letters *a* through *z* . . .
]	the end of the character class . . .
)	the end of the group . . .
\/	the final path separator.

A Perl-specific feature found in the replacement expression here is \U, which changes the back reference $1 to uppercase. This is really for readability more than anything else—Windows isn't case sensitive when it comes to paths and drive letters.

URLS AND PATHS

PHP

```
html>
<head><title>2-5 Translating Unix Paths to DOS paths</title></head>
<body>
<form action="recipe2-5.php" method="post">
<input type="text" name="value" value="<? print $_POST['value']; ?>"/><br/>
<input type="submit" value="Submit" /><br/><br/>
<?php
if ( $_SERVER['REQUEST_METHOD'] == "POST" )
{
    $mystr = $_POST['value'];
    if ( $newstr = preg_replace( "/^\/cygdrive\/([a-z])\//", "$1:\\", $mystr ) )
    {
        $newstr = preg_replace( "/\//", "\\", $newstr );
        print "<b>$newstr</b>";
    }
}
?>
</form>
</body>
</html>
```

How It Works

See "How It Works" under the Perl example for a breakdown of the search expression.

2-6. Extracting Directories from Full Paths

These expressions use back references to capture a directory name from a full path name.

Perl

```
#!/usr/bin/perl -w
use strict;

my $mystr = $ARGV[0] || die "Please supply a parameter";

$mystr =~ s/^\/(.*)\/[^\/]+$/\/$1/;
print $mystr . "\n";
```

How It Works

This Perl recipe uses the word boundary character class \b and a back reference to isolate a file path and, with the back reference, assign it to a variable.

You can break down the expression like this:

^	the beginning line anchor, followed by . . .
\/	a slash, then . . .
(	the beginning of a group that captures . . .
.	any character . . .
*	found zero, one, or many times . . .
)	and ending before . . .
\/	a slash that's followed by . . .
[	a class of characters . . .
^	that doesn't contain . . .
\/	a slash . . .
]	the end of the character class . . .
+	where the character class exists one or more times, followed by . . .
$	the end of the line.

The group in parentheses is referenced by the back reference $1. The group will match everything up to the first slash from left to right that doesn't have another slash after it—which will capture the directory. This isn't an exact science but will give an output similar to the dirname command found on many Unix machines.

PHP

```
<html>
<head><title>2-6 Extracting directiories from full paths</title></head>
<body>
<form action="recipe2-6.php" method="post">
<input type="text" name="value" value="<? print $_POST ['value']; ?>"/><br/>
<input type="submit" value="Submit" /><br/><br/>
<?php
if ( $_SERVER['REQUEST_METHOD'] == "POST" )
{
    $mystr = $_POST['value'];
    if ( ereg( '^\/(.*)\/([^\/]+$|$)', $mystr, $matches ) )
    {
        echo "The directory is:  /$matches[1]";
    }
}
?>
</form>
</body>
</html>
```

How It Works

The expression found in the PHP recipe is a little different from the expression found in the Perl expression; in this example, ereg() is being used, which is based on the extended POSIX regular expression implementation. Instead of using a word anchor here, I'm using line anchors for brevity. Here it is:

^	the beginning of the line, followed by . . .
\/	a slash, then . . .
(	the beginning of the group that captures . . .
.	any character . . .
*	found zero, one, or many times . . .
)	the end of the group, followed by . . .
\/	a slash, then . . .
(	the beginning of a group that contains . . .
[	a character class . . .
^	that doesn't include . . .
\/	a slash . . .
]	the end of the character class . . .

+	found at least one time, followed by . . .
$	the end of the line . . .
|	or . . .
$	the end of the line (without the [^\/]+ stuff).

If you use preg_match() instead of ereg(), you can use the expression from the Perl recipe.

Shell Scripting

```
$ echo filename | sed 's/^\/\(.*\)\/[^\/]\+$/\/\1/'
```

How It Works

When running this command in the shell, substitute filename with the name of the file. Remember to use single quotes around the sed expression to stop the shell from making variable substitutions and other interpretations.

See "How It Works" under the Perl example for a walk-through of this expression, with the only differences being the escaped (,), and +.

Vim

```
%s/^\/\(.*\)\/[^\/]\+$/\/\1/
```

How It Works

To walk through this expression, see "How It Works" under the Perl example. Remember that you escape the special characters (,), and + in Vim with a \.

Variations

The most common variation on this recipe is to modify it so it works with Windows-style path names. This entails using a \ as a directory separator instead of a /. When you use a \ in an expression, you must escape it. The Perl version of the expression becomes \b\\(.*)\\([^\\]+\b|$). Of course, if you go with a DOS-style directory separator, you'll probably want to specify the drive letter at the beginning of the expression, like this: \b[A-Z]\:\\(.*)\\([^\\]+\b|$). A combination expression that does both DOS- and Unix-style paths is /\b([a-zA-z]:\\|\/)(.*)[\\\/]([^\\\/]+\b|$).

2-7. Extracting Filenames from Full Paths

This recipe extracts what looks like a filename from a full path. It makes an assumption that anything after the last directory separator (in this case /) is the name of a file.

Perl

```perl
#!/usr/bin/perl -w
use strict;

my $mystr = $ARGV[0] || die "Please supply a parameter";

if ( $mystr =~ s/^\/.+\/([^\/]+)$/$1/ )
{
    print "'" . $mystr  . "'\n";
}
else
{
    print "No filename found!\n";
}
```

How It Works

The negation character ^ found in the character class [^\/] is an important element in this expression. Here's a breakdown of the expression:

^	the beginning of the line, followed by . . .
\/	a slash, then . . .
.	any character . . .
+	found one or more times, up to . . .
\/	a slash, followed by . . .
(	the beginning of the group that will capture the filename and contains . . .
[	a character class that contains . . .
^	anything that isn't . . .
\/	a slash . . .
]	the end of the character class . . .
+	found one or more times . . .
)	the end of the group, which goes up to . . .
$	the end of the line . . .

The text that matches the group is referenced with the back reference $1 in the previous script and is used to assign that value to a variable. The variable will then contain everything after the last slash, from right to left, in the string that doesn't have another slash after it.

PHP

```
<html>
<head><title></title></head>
<body>
<form action="recipe2-7.php" method="post">
<input type="text" name="value" value="<? print $_POST ['value']; ?>"/><br/>
<input type="submit" value="Submit" /><br/><br/>
<?php
if ( $_SERVER['REQUEST_METHOD'] == "POST" )
{
    $mystr = $_POST['value'];
    if ( ereg( '^\/.*\/([^\/]+)$', $mystr, $matches ) )
    {
        echo "The file is:  $matches[1]";
    }
    else
    {
        echo "<b>No file found here.</b>";
    }
}
?>
</form>
</body>
</html>
```

How It Works

The expression used in this PHP recipe, even though it uses ereg(), is the same as the expression in the Perl recipe. Refer to the Perl recipe's "How It Works" section to see how the expression breaks down into pieces.

Shell Scripting

```
$ echo filename | sed ' s/^\/.*\/\([^\/]\+\)$/\1/'
```

How It Works

To run this on the command line, substitute filename with a full file path.

Refer to "How It Works" under the Perl example to see how this expression breaks down. Remember to escape the characters (,), and +.

Vim

```
:%s/^\/.*\/\([^\/]\+\)$/\1/
```

How It Works

See "How It Works" under the Perl example—the only difference is the escape character \ before the (,), and + characters in PCRE, which are grouping characters and a qualifier, respectively.

2-8. Extracting File Extensions from Full Paths

This recipe finds a file extension, based on an assumption that a two- to four-character string after the last . in a full path is an extension. Given a path such as /your/directory/here/file.ext, the recipe will pull out ext from the string.

Perl

```perl
#!/usr/bin/perl -w
use strict;

my $mystr = $ARGV[0] || die "Please supply a parameter";

if ( $mystr =~ s/^.+\.(\w{2,4})$/$1/ )
{
    print "'" . $mystr  . "'\n";
}
else
{
    print "No file extension found!\n";
}
```

How It Works

This expression makes a few assumptions to identify a file extension. One assumption is that a file extension is a two- to four-character group, such as sh, txt, and text. Another assumption is that this group of characters must appear after the last period or dot in a string.

You can break the expression down like this:

^	the beginning of the line, followed by . . .
.	any character . . .
+	found at least one time, followed by . . .
\.	a literal dot (.) . . .
(	the beginning of the group that captures . . .
\w	any alphanumeric character . . .
{2,4}	found between two and four times . . .
)	the end of the group, and finally . . .
$	the end of the line.

This expression includes the range qualifier {n,n}. When two numbers are specified in a range inside braces and separated by a comma, the numbers are used as the minimum and maximum numbers of time in which the preceding expression can appear. The range is inclusive, so in this case three occurrences of any character (.) will match successfully.

URLS AND PATHS

PHP

```
<html>
<head><title></title></head>
<body>
<form action="recipe2-8.php" method="post">
<input type="text" name="value" value="<? print $_POST['value']; ?>"/><br/>
<input type="submit" value="Submit" /><br/><br/>
<?php
if ( $_SERVER['REQUEST_METHOD'] == "POST" )
{
    $mystr = $_POST['value'];
    if ( ereg( '^.+\.([[:alpha:]]{2,4})$', $mystr, $matches ) )
    {
        echo "The extension is:  $matches[1]";
    }
    else
    {
        echo "<b>I didn't find a valid expression.</b>";
    }
}
?>
</form>
</body>
</html>
```

How It Works

The expression used to match the string in the PHP recipe is similar to the Perl recipe, with the exception of the character class used. The PHP recipe uses ereg(), which uses POSIX-extended regular expressions.

Here's the breakdown of the PHP recipe with the difference called out in bold:

^	the beginning of the line, followed by . . .
.	any character . . .
+	found at least one time (one or more), followed by . . .
\.	a literal dot (.) . . .
(	the beginning of the group that captures . . .
[[:alpha:]]	any alphanumeric character . . .
{2,4}	found between two and four times . . .
)	the end of the group, and finally . . .
$	the end of the line.

Shell Scripting

```
$ echo filename | sed 's/^.\+\.\([A-Za-z-9_]\{2,4\}\)$/\1/'
```

How It Works

See "How It Works" under the Perl example. In addition to the escaped +, (,), {, and } characters, the \w character class is replaced with [A-Za-z0-9_].

Vim

```
%s/^.\+\.\(\w\{2,4\}\)$/\1/
```

How It Works

See "How It Works" under the Perl example, but remember to add the escape character \ to give +, (,), {, and } their special meanings.

Variations

One of the changes you may want to make to the expression is to do away with the assumption that a file extension is only two to four characters in length. Maybe you want to say "at least two characters," in which case you can simply drop off the last number in the range like this: {2,}. If the range qualifier doesn't contain a second number, the expression will match anything greater than the first number. (The comma must be present; otherwise it will match two instances of the preceding expression.)

Or, perhaps instead of using a character class to specify alphanumeric characters, you may use ranges instead, such as [A-Za-z0-9]. Using ranges yields a longer expression and sometimes makes them more difficult to read. The benefit is that the expression is more portable because you don't have to worry about character class implementations between the different regular expression flavors.

■**Note** Ranges such as A–z work in capturing both A–Z and a–z and also other characters such as [, \,], ^, _, and ` in some regular expression implementations. However, a–Z won't work at all.

■**See Also** 2-6, 2-7

2-9. Replacing URLs with Links

This recipe locates a URL inside a string and reformats the URL to be inside an `<a>` tag to create a link. Given a string such as `Link to my URL:  http://www.mydomain.com`, the result will be `Link to my URL:  <a href="http://www.mydomain.com">http://www.mydomain.com</a>`.

Perl

```
#!/usr/bin/perl -w
use strict;

my $mystr = $ARGV[0] || die "Please supply a parameter";

$mystr =~ s/\b(http:\/\/\S+[^-.,\"\';: ])\b/<a href="$1">$1<\/a>/g;
print $mystr . "\n";
```

How It Works

You may look at this expression and wonder why the character class `[^-.,"';:]` is included in the expression (the double and single quotes are escaped, so Perl leaves them alone). While I was testing this expression, my first crack at it didn't include this, and I found that a line in the file that said

`This is my URL:  http://www.example.com.`

was translated into the following:

`This is my URL:  <a href="http://www.example.com.">http://www.example.com.</a>`

This wasn't the intention of the expression. The expression ends in `\b`, so why did the expression capture the `.`?

This happened because the `\b` also matches the end of the line, so the sequence `\S+\b` matches also a `.` (which isn't whitespace) followed by the end of the line. The character class `[^-.,"';:]` was added to leave punctuation alone.

You can break down the expression as follows:

`\b`	word boundary, followed by . . .
`http`	an *h*, *t*, *t*, and *p*, then . . .
`\:`	a colon . . .
`\/`	a slash, then . . .
`\/`	another slash, followed by . . .
`\S`	a nonwhite space character . . .
`+`	found one or more times . . .
`[^`	a character class that *doesn't* contain . . .

-	a hyphen (put right after the negation character so it's not a range) . . .
.	a period . . .
,	a comma . . .
\"	a double quote . . .
\'	a single quote . . .
;	a semicolon . . .
:	a colon, and . . .
<space>	a space . . .
]	the end of the character class . . .
)	the end of the group . . .
\b	followed by a word boundary.

URLS AND PATHS

PHP

```
<html>
<head><title>2-9 Replacing URLs with links</title></head>
<body>
<form action="recipe2-9.php" method="post">
<input type="text" name="value" value="<? print $_POST ['value']; ?>"/><br/>
<input type="submit" value="Submit" /><br/><br/>
<?php
if ( $_SERVER['REQUEST_METHOD'] == "POST" )
{
    $mystr = $_POST['value'];
    if ( $mylinkedstr = preg_replace( "/\b(http:\/\/\S+[^-.,\"\';: ])\b/",
        "<a href='\\1'>\\1</a>", $mystr ) )
    {
        print "$mylinkedstr";
    }
    else
    {
        print "<b>I didn't find a valid expression.</b>";
    }
}
?>
</form>
</body>
</html>
```

How It Works

The PHP recipe uses `preg_replace()` instead of the POSIX-based `ereg_replace()` because of the availability of noncapturing parentheses. Making the replacement is still possible using `ereg_replace`, and you can find the expressions for both the search and the replace in the "Variations" section.

Refer to "How It Works" in the Perl section to see how the regular expression works.

Shell Scripting

```
$ echo string | \
    sed 's/\<\(http:\/\/[^[:space:]]\+[^-",.:; ]\)\>/<a href=\"\1\">\1<\/a>/g'
```

How It Works

To see how this expression breaks down, refer to "How It Works" under the Perl example—just remember to escape (,), and +. The only other difference is that the \S character class isn't supported by sed and is replaced by [^[:space:]].

You can replace the word *string* in the previous example with a string containing a URL.

Vim

```
:%s/\<\(http:\/\/\S\+[^-,.'":; ]\)\>/<a href="\1">\1<\/a>/g
```

How It Works

To see how this expression breaks down, refer to "How It Works" under the Perl example.

Variations

One variation on the PHP recipe is to use the `ereg_replace` function instead. Since the `ereg_replace` function doesn't support noncapturing groups, you have to take the beginning and end whitespace groups into account when you're making your replacement. The search expression, since it uses the longer POSIX syntax for character classes, is `(^|[[:space:]])` `(http\:\/\/[[:alpha:].]+\/?[^[:space:]]*)([[:space:]]|$)`. The replace expression is `\\1<a href='\\2'>\\2</a>\\3`.

▪ **See Also** 2-10

2-10. Replacing E-mail Addresses with Links

Similar to recipe 2-9, this recipe searches a string for something that's formatted like an e-mail address. When it finds an e-mail address, it creates a link to the address using the `<a>` HTML tag. Given the string `My address is user@mydomain.com`, the result will be `My address is <a href='mailto:user@mydomain.com'>user@mydomain.com</a>`.

Perl

```
#!/usr/bin/perl -w
use strict;

my $mystr = $ARGV[0] || die "Please supply a parameter";

$mystr =~ s/\b(\w+@[\w.]+)\b/<a href="mailto:$1">$1<\/a>/g;
print $mystr . "\n";
```

How It Works

The expression group used for the e-mail address is basic in this example. For a much more complicated and thorough expression for e-mail addresses, see recipe 4-11.

Here's the expression broken down into parts:

\b	a word boundary, such as a space or beginning of a line, followed by . . .
(	the beginning of a capturing group that contains . . .
\w	a "word" character class . . .
+	found at least on time, until an . . .
@	at sign, followed by . . .
[	a character class that includes . . .
\w	a "word character" . . .
.	or a period (dot) . . .
]	the end of the group . . .
+	found at least one time . . .
\b	followed by a word boundary.

PHP

```
<html>
<head><title>2-10 Replacing email addresses with links</title></head>
<body>
```

URLS AND PATHS

```
<form action="recipe2-10.php" method="post">
<input type="text" name="value" value="<? print $_POST['value']; ?>"/><br/>
<input type="submit" value="Submit" /><br/><br/>
<?php
if ( $_SERVER['REQUEST_METHOD'] == "POST" )
{
    $mystr = $_POST['value'];
    $mylinkedstr = preg_replace( "/(?:(?<=\s)|(?<=^))(\w+@[\w.]+)(?=\s|$)/",
        "<a href='mailto:\\1'>\\1</a>", $mystr );
    print "$mylinkedstr";
}
?>
</form>
</body>
</html>
```

How It Works

The PHP recipe here uses PCRE supplied by preg_replace(). The expression used in the Perl recipe would work fine, but I'm showing this one to demonstrate how to use look-arounds.

Here's the expression broken down into parts:

(?:	the beginning of a noncapturing group that contains . . .
(?<=	a positive look-behind containing . . .
\s	whitespace . . .
)	the end of the positive look-behind . . .
|	or . . .
(?<=	a positive look-behind containing . . .
^	the beginning of the line, followed by . . .
)	the end of the positive look-behind . . .
)	the end of a group . . .
(	a group that captures . . .
\w	a word character . . .
+	at least one time, up to . . .
@	an at sign, followed by . . .
\w	a word character . . .
+	found one or more times, then . . .
)	the end of a group . . .

(?=	a positive look-ahead group containing . . .
\s	whitespace . . .
|	or . . .
$	the end of the line . . .
)	the end of a group.

Vim

```
%s/\<\([0-9A-Za-z_.]\+@[0-9A-Za-z_.]\+\)\>/<a href="mailto:\1">\1<\/a>/g
```

How It Works

You can use this regular expression to replace an e-mail address with an HTML link version of the address in a file.

You can break down the expression used in vi as follows:

\<	a word anchor, followed by . . .
\(	the beginning of a group that captures . . .
[0-9A-Za-z_]	a character class that includes letters and numbers, underscores (_) and dots (.) . . .
\+	found one or more times, up to . . .
@	an at sign, followed by . . .
[0-9A-Za-z_]	the same character class as previously . . .
\+	found one or more times . . .
\)	the end of a group . . .
\>	the ending word anchor.

2-11. Searching for Multiple File Types

You can use this recipe for searching directories for files that may be related but have different extensions. Some examples are text files that end in .txt, .text, and .TXT. This recipe will match file.txt, my.file.txt, file.text, and file.TXT.

Perl

```
#!/usr/bin/perl -w
use strict;

opendir( CURDIR, '.' ) || die "The ship can't take much more of this, captain!\n";

my @files = readdir CURDIR;
closedir CURDIR;

foreach my $file ( @files )
{
    if ( $file =~ /^[-a-z0-9._]+\.te?xt$/i )
    {
        print "$file\n";
    }
}
```

How It Works

This Perl script loads the names of the files in a directory in an array. For each member of the array, the script attempts a match against the filename; if the match is successful, it prints the name of the file.

This expression is fairly basic; it breaks down like this:

^	the beginning of the string, followed by . . .
[-a-z0-9._]	a character class that includes letters, numbers, hyphens (-), dots (.), and underscores (_) . . .
+	one or more times, up to . . .
\.	a literal dot, then . . .
t	a *t*, then . . .
e	an *e* . . .
?	found at most one time . . .
x	the letter *x*, then . . .
t	the letter *t* . . .
$	the end of the string.

PHP

```
<html>
<head><title>2-11 Searching for multiple file types</title></head>
<body>
<form action="recipe2-11.php" method="post">
<input type="submit" value="Find my text files" /><br/><br/>
<?php
if ( $_SERVER['REQUEST_METHOD'] == "POST" )
{
    $dir = opendir( '/var/tmp' );
    while ( $file = readdir( $dir ) )
    {
        if ( preg_match( '/^[-a-z0-9._]+\.te?xt$/i', $file ) )
        {
            print "Found file:   <b>$file</b><br />";
        }
    }
}
?>
</form>
</body>
</html>
```

How It Works

The PHP recipe uses preg_match(), which uses PCRE. The expression is the same as the expression given in the Perl recipe.

Shell Scripting

```
$ find . -iregex '^\.\/[-a-z0-9_.]+\.(te?xt|TXT)$ '
```

How It Works

When using regular expressions with find, remember that the expression must match the complete filename, including the directory name. When you're using find to view files in the current directory, the names will start with ./. Hence, the only modification to the expression is the addition of \.\/ at the beginning of the expression.

2-12. Changing the Extensions of Multiple Files

You can use this recipe to rename multiple files that have different extensions to have the same extension. For example, you could use this recipe when several text files exist in a directory but have slightly different extensions such as .txt, .TXT, or .text. This recipe shows you how to rename them to all have .txt extensions.

Perl

```perl
#!/usr/bin/perl -w
use strict;

opendir( CURDIR, '.' ) || die "The ship can't take much more of this, captain!\n";

my @files = readdir CURDIR;
closedir CURDIR;

foreach my $file ( @files )
{
    if ( $file =~ /^[-A-Za-z0-9._]+\.(?:txt|TXT|text)$/ )
    {
        # rename the file
        my $newfilename = $file;
        $newfilename =~ s/^([-A-Za-z0-9._]+)\.(?:te?xt|TXT|)/$1\.txt/;
        rename $file, $newfilename || die "Could not rename file '" .
            $file . "'\n";
    }
}
```

How It Works

In this recipe, the capturing parentheses wrap the filename and leave the extension alone. The grouping around the extension is modified with a (?: to become a noncapturing forward-looking group, so you don't have to worry about capturing the wrong text.

^	the beginning of the line...
(	the beginning of a group that contains...
[	a character class that contains...
-	a hyphen...
A-z	A through z...
0-9	0 through 9...
.	a period...
_	an underscore...

]	the end of the character class...
+	found one or more times...
)	the end of the group...
\.	a literal period or dot...
(?:	a noncapturing group that contains...
t	a t...
e	an e...
?	found zero or one time...
x	an x...
t	a t...
|	or...
TXT	T, X, T...
)	the end of the noncapturing group...
$	the end of the line.

PHP

```
<html>
<head><title>2-12 Changing the extensions of multiple files</title></head>
<body>
<form action="recipe2-12.php" method="post">
<input type="submit" value="Rename my files" /><br/><br/>
<?php
if ( $_SERVER['REQUEST_METHOD'] == "POST" )
{
    $dirname = "/var/tmp";
    $dir = opendir( $dirname );
    while ( $file = readdir( $dir ) )
    {
        {
            if ( preg_match( '/^[-A-Za-z0-9_.]+\.(?:TXT|te?xt)$/', $file ) )
            {
                $newfile = preg_replace( '/^([-A-Za-z0-9_.]+)\.(?:TXT|te?xt)$/',
                '\1.txt', $file
);

                rename( "$dirname/$file", "$dirname/$newfile" )
                    or die ( "Cannot rename file." );
```

```
                    print "<b>File \"$dirname/$file\" renamed to
\"$dirname/$newfile\"</b><br />";
                }
                else
                {
                    print "<b>No match found in file \"$file\"</b><br/>";
                }
            }
        }
    }
?>
</form>
</body>
</html>
```

How It Works

To see how this expression works, refer to "How It Works" under the Perl recipe. If you were to use ereg() instead of preg_match(), the noncapturing group for the file extension would be replaced with a normal group.

2-13. Making URL Query String Substitutions

This recipe demonstrates how to replace a query string in a URL. The assumption is that everything after the first ? from left to right is the query string. Variations on this recipe allow you to replace single parameter and variable pairs, making sure you're inside a query string.

Perl

```perl
#!/usr/bin/perl -w
use strict;

my $mystr = $ARGV[0] || die "Please supply a parameter";

$mystr =~ s/^(https?:\/\/(?:[A-Za-z0-9][-A-Za-z0-9]+\.)+[A-Za-z]{2,6}⤶
(?::[0-9]+)?\/[-\w.\/]+)(?:\?[-⤶
\w:@=&\$.+!*'()"]+)$/$1?new=parameter/g;
print "'" . $mystr . "'\n";
```

How It Works

The keys to this expression are the character classes that define which characters can appear in the string. These character classes make sure the URL looks like a valid one and are based on the request for comment (RFC) that describes which characters are allowed in a URL and which characters are allowed in a domain name.

This expression, since it's so long, is best if it's broken down into the pieces of the URL. The part of the URL that searches for http:// or https:// is as follows:

http   the letters *h*, *t*, *t*, and *p*, then . . .

s   the letter *s* . . .

?   found at most one time, followed by . . .

:   a colon, then . . .

\/   a slash and . . .

\/   another slash.

After the schema part of the URL comes the domain section. The domain section is (?:[A-Za-z0-9][-A-Za-z0-9]+\.)+[A-Za-z]{2,6}. This is everything from the schema part of the URL to the optional port part. You can break down this expression into the following:

(?:   a noncapturing group that contains . . .

[..]   the domain character classes . . .

+   found one or more times, then . . .

\.   a dot . . .

)+   where this group can be found one or more times, then . . .

[A-Za-z] a letter . . .

{2,6}   found two to six times.

The domain character classes are the concatenation of [A-Za-z][-A-Za-z0-9], since domain labels must begin with a letter and then end with a letter, number, or hyphen. The \w character class isn't used here because although it will work most of the time, it's too broad. The \w character class not only matches letters and numbers but also matches an underscore, which isn't a valid part of a label in a domain name.

You can declare the port in a URL after the domain name and before the first directory separator (/). A colon (:) separates the port from the domain name.

(?:   a noncapturing group that contains . . .

:   a colon, followed by . . .

[0-9]   a number . . .

+   that can be found one or more times . . .

)?   where the entire group can appear at most once.

After the first directory separator, file and directory names, as well as directory separators, can appear until the first ?. The expression used to match this is \/[-\w.\/]+, which means the following:

\/   the first directory separator, followed by . . .

[...]   the character class that matches word characters, underscores, and so on . . .

*   found zero, one or many times.

After the optional filename and directory names comes the query string portion of the URL. Since the query string isn't used in the replacement, it's enclosed in noncapturing parentheses. The expression is as follows:

(?:   up to the noncapturing group that contains . . .

\?   the question mark, followed by . . .

[...]   a character class that contains legal URL characters . . .

+   found one or more times up to . . .

)   the end of a group . . .

$ the end.

The legal URL characters are letters, numbers, and the special characters /, ;, ?, :, @, =, &, $, -, _, ., +, !, *, ', (,), and ". The character class to match these is [-\w:@=&\$.+!*'()"].

PHP

```
<html>
<head><title>2-13 Making URL query string substitutions</title></head>
<body>
<form action="recipe2-13.php" method="post">
<input type="text" name="value" value="<? print $_POST['value']; ?>"/><br/>
<input type="submit" value="Submit" /><br/><br/>
<?php
if ( $_SERVER['REQUEST_METHOD'] == "POST" )
{
    $myurl = $_POST['value'];
    $newurl = preg_replace( "/^(https?:\/\/(?:[A-Za-z0-9][-A-Za-z0-9]+\.)↵
+[A-Za-z]{2,6}(?::[0-9]+)?\/[-\w.\/]*)↵
(?:\?[-\w:@=&$.+!*'()\"]+)$/","$1?new=parameter", $myurl );
    print "<b>$newurl</b><br/>";
}
?>
</form>
</body>
</html>
```

How It Works

To learn how the expression in this recipe works, refer to "How It Works" under the Perl recipe. The only difference between the two expressions is that the double quote in the expression must be escaped.

Shell Scripting

```
$ echo url | sed 's/^\(https\?:\/\/\([A-Za-z0-9][-A-Za-z0-9]\+\.\)\+[A-Za-z]\{2,6\}↵
\(:[0-9]\+\)\?\/[-A-Za-z0-9_.\/]*\)\(?[-_A-Za-z0-9:@=&$.+!*()"]\+\)$/↵
\1?new=parameter/'
```

How It Works

The GNU sed command doesn't support noncapturing groups, so they were removed from the search expression. However, since back references work from the outside in, this doesn't become much of an issue.

See "How It Works" under the Vim example for additional differences, and see "How It Works" under the Perl example for a breakdown of this expression.

Vim

```
:%s/^\(https\?:\/\/\%([A-Za-z0-9][-A-Za-z0-9]\+\.\)\+[A-Za-z]\{2,6\}\%↵
(:[0-9]\+\)\?\/[-A-Za-z0-9_.\/]*\)\%(?[-_A-Za-z0-9:@=&$.+!*'()"]\+\)$/↵
\1?new=parameter/
```

How It Works

In addition to the escaped (,), ?, {, }, and + characters, two differences between this expression and the PCRE expressions exist in this recipe. The first is that the syntax for a noncapturing group in Vim is \%(...\) instead of the PCRE (?:...). The other difference is the \w inside the character class [and] has been replaced by A-Za-z0-9_.

A similar expression has been broken down in "How It Works" under the Perl example.

2-14. Rewriting URLs

This recipe allows you to change the directory and filename of a URL but keep the domain name and query string. This can be handy if you're hiding path and filename information from your user.

Perl

```perl
#!/usr/bin/perl -w
use strict;

my $mystr = $ARGV[0] || die "Please supply a parameter";

$mystr =~ s/(^https?:\/\/(?:[A-z0-9][-A-z0-9]+\.)+[A-z]{2,4}↵
(?::[0-9]+)?\/)(?:[-\w.\/]+)(\?[-↵
\w:@=&\$.+!*'()"]+)$/$1different\/path\/file.php$2/g;
print "'" . $mystr . "'\n";
```

How It Works

For a detailed walk-through of this expression, see the explanations in recipe 2-13. The grouping has been changed in this version of the expression to group up to the first directory separator and then again after the first question mark to grab the query string.

Shell Scripting

```
$ echo url | sed 's/\(^https\?:\/\/\([A-z0-9][-A-z0-9]+\.\)\+[A-z]\{2,4\}↵
\(:[0-9]\+\)\?\/\)\([-A-z0-9_.\/]\+\)↵
\(?[A-z0-9_:@=&\$.+!*()]\+\)$/\1different\/path\/file.php\2/'
```

How It Works

See "How It Works" under the Perl example in this recipe for a walk-through of this expression—escape (,), ?, {, }, and +, and remove the noncapturing groups.

Vim

```
%s/^\(https\?:\/\/\%([A-z0-9][-A-z0-9]\+\.\)\+[A-z]\{2,4\}↵
\%(:[0-9]\+\)\?\/\)\%([-A-z0-9_.\/]\+\)↵
(?[A-z0-9_:@=&\$.+!*'()"]\+\)$/\1different\/path\/file.php\2/
```

How It Works

See "How It Works" under the Perl example in recipe 2-13. In addition to the escaped (,), ?, {, }, and + characters, two differences between this expression and the PCRE expressions exist in recipe 2-13. The syntax for a noncapturing group in Vim is \%(...\) instead of the PCRE (?:...), and the \w inside the character class [and] has been replaced by A-z0-9_.

2-15. Replacing IP Addresses in URLs

This recipe focuses on replacing an Internet Protocol (IP) address in a URL with another string, presumably a hostname. This recipe will replace `http://192.168.0.10/index.html` with `http://www.example.com/index.html`.

Perl

```
#!/usr/bin/perl -w
use strict;

my $mystr = $ARGV[0] || die "Please supply a parameter";

$mystr =~ s/^(https?:\/\/)(?:((25[0-5]|2[0-4][0-9]|1?[0-9]{2}|[0-9])\.){3}↵
(25[0-5]|2[0-4][0-9]|1?[0-9]{2}|[0-9])/$1host.example.com/;

print "'" . $mystr . "'\n";
```

How It Works

Before I get into the rest of the expression, I'll walk through the expression to make sure the IP address in the URL is valid.

(?:	a nongrouping expression that has . . .
(	a group that contains . . .
(...)	a group that defines an octet in an IP address, found before . . .
\.	a dot . . .
)	the end of the group . . .
{3}	where the octet definition is found three times . . .
(...)	the same group that defines the octet.

The expression inside the group that defines an octet is `25[0-5]|2[0-4][0-9]|1?[0-9]{2}|[0-9]`. The expression matches any number from 0 to 255.

25[0-5]	matches 250–255 . . .
|	or . . .
2[0-4][0-9]	matches 200–249 . . .
|	or . . .
1?[0-9]{2}	matches 00–199 . . .
|	or . . .
[0-9]	matches, well, 0–9.

You can see that in this case all the bases are covered between 0 and 255. The expression replaces the IP address with a hostname (provided one is supplied in the replacement text) and remembers the protocol (either http or https in this case) with the back reference.

PHP

```
<html>
<head><title>2-15 Replacing IP addresses in URLs</title></head>
<body>
<form action="recipe2-15.php" method="post">
Enter URL with IP address here:
<input type="text" name="value" value="<? print $_POST ['value']; ?>"/><br/>
<input type="submit" value="Submit" /><br/><br/>
<?php
if ( $_SERVER['REQUEST_METHOD'] == "POST" )
{
    $myurl = $_POST['value'];
    $newstr = preg_replace( '/^(https?:\/\/)(?:((25[0-5]|2[0-4][0-9]| ↵
1?[0-9]{2}|[0-9])\.){3}(25[0-5]|2[0-4][0-9]|1?[0-9]{2}|[0-9])/',
          '$1host.example.com/', $myurl );
      print "<b>$newstr</b><br/>";
}
?>
</form>
</body>
</html>
```

How It Works

The PHP recipe shown here uses PCRE brought to you by preg_replace(). To walk through this expression, visit "How It Works" under the Perl example for this recipe.

Shell Scripting

```
$ echo 'http://192.168.0.0/moo.com' | \
  sed 's/^\(https\?:\/\/\)\(\(25[0-5]\|2[0-4][0-9]\|1\?[0-9]\{2\}\)\| ↵
[0-9]\)\.\)\{3\}\(25[0-5]\|2[0-4][0-9]\|1\?[0-9]\{2\}\|[09]\)/ ↵
\1host.example.com/'
```

How It Works

See "How It Works" under the Perl example—remember that the noncapturing groups are removed and that the characters (,), {, }, |, and ? are escaped.

Vim

```
:%s/^\(https\?:\/\/\)\%(\%(25[0-5]\|2[0-4][0-9]\|1\?[0-9]\{2}\| ⏎
[0-9]\)\)\.\)\{3}\%(25[0-5]\|2[0-4][0-9]\|1\?[0-9]\{2}\|[0-9]\)/ ⏎
\1host.example.com/
```

How It Works

This expression, or one a lot like it, is broken down in "How It Works" under the Perl expression. The differences are escaped with (,), {, }, |, +, and ?.

## CHAPTER 3

CSV and Tab-Delimited Files

The recipes in this chapter focus on working with tab-delimited and comma-separated-value (CSV) files. These handy recipes allow you to find lines with a specific number of fields, and they even give you the ability to transform tab-delimited files to CSV, and vice versa.

3-1. Finding Bad CSV Records

You can use this recipe to isolate records in a CSV file that don't have the correct number of
fields in them, which can sometimes be caused by commas appearing in fields, and so on.

Perl

```
#!/usr/bin/perl -w
use strict;

open( FILE, $ARGV[0] ) || die "Cannot open file!";

my $i = 0;

while ( <FILE> )
{
    $i++;
    next if /^([^,"]+|"([^"]|\\")*")(,([^,"]+|"([^"]|\\")*")){2}$/;
    print $_;
}

close( FILE );
```

How It Works

The Perl recipe shown here prints all lines in a file that don't have three CSV fields. You can
change the range qualifier {2} to match any number of fields, where the range qualifier is the
number of total fields minus one.

The expression repeats that same grouping twice, ([^",]+|"([^"]|\\")*"). You can break
this group down into two parts as follows:

[^,"]   a character class that isn't a comma or a double quote . . .

+   found one or more times . . .

| or . . .

"   a quote, followed by . . .

(a group containing . . .

[^"]   a character class that isn't another quote . . .

| or . . .

\\"   an escaped quote . . .

)   the end of the group . . .

*   where the group is found none or many times, up to . . .

"   another quote.

This represents one field in a CSV file and appears in parentheses that group it. The first field is followed by a certain number of fields, where a comma precedes each field after the first one.

To make this expression a little more understandable, replace the field expression ([^,"]+|"([^"]|\\")*") with X. You'll get ^X(,X){2}$—so you have one field, followed by two more for a total of three CSV fields.

PHP

```
<html>
<head><title>3-1 Finding bad CSV records</title></head>
<body>
<form action="recipe3-1.php" method="post">
<textarea name="records" cols="20" rows="10"></textarea><br/>
<input type="submit" value="Find the bad CSV records" /><br/><br/>
<?php
if ( $_SERVER['REQUEST_METHOD'] == "POST" )
{
    $lines = explode( "\n", $_POST['records'] );
    foreach ($lines as $line)
    {
        if ( ! preg_match( "/^([^,\"]+|\"([^\"]|\\\")*\")↵
(,([^,\"]+|\"([^\"]|\\\")*\")){2}$/", $line ) )
        {
            print "<b>$line</b><br/>";
        }
    }
}
?>
</form>
</body>
</html>
```

How It Works

Since the previous PHP recipe uses the Perl-Compatible Regular Expression (PCRE) preg_match() function, see the Perl recipe's "How It Works" section to gain an understanding of this expression. Keep in mind that in the PHP recipe, double quotes in the expression are escaped with a \.

The PHP recipe iterates through lines pasted into a text area and prints the lines that have three CSV fields in them. To print a different number of lines, modify the range qualifier {2} to be the number of fields you're looking for minus one.

Shell Scripting

```
$ grep -v '^\(([^,"]\+\|"\([^"]\|\\"\)*"\)\)\(,[^,"]\+\|"↵
\([^"]\|\\"\)*"\)\){2\}$' filename
```

How It Works

To walk through the expression in this recipe, visit the "How It Works" section for the Perl recipe.

The -v parameter tells grep to print lines that don't match the expression, so by using this expression you can find lines in a file that don't match the number of CSV fields asked for in the expression.

Vim

```
/^\([^,"]\+\|"\([^"]\|\\"\)*"\)\(,\([^,"]\+\|"\([^"]\|\\"\)*"\)\)\{2\}$
```

How It Works

Refer to "How It Works" under the Perl expression to see how this expression breaks down. Remember to give the (,), +, and | characters their special meaning by escaping them with a \.

The Vim expression here also works differently: it finds *valid* records while the others used options to show only lines that didn't match the search. I looked, but I found no such option in Vim. To find lines that don't match, simply modify the expression to find lines that don't have three fields in them. Change the 2 to a 3 in the qualifier, for instance.

Variations

To increase performance with the Perl recipe, you can use noncapturing parentheses. I didn't use them in the initial recipe because they make the expressions difficult to read. Using noncapturing parentheses, the expression ([^",]+|"([^"]|\\")*") becomes (?:[^",]+|"(?:[^"]|\\")*").

3-2. Finding Bad Tab-Delimited Records

You can use this recipe to find records in a tab-delimited file that have five fields in them.

Perl

```perl
#!/usr/bin/perl -w
use strict;

open( FILE, $ARGV[0] ) || die "Cannot open file!";

my $i = 0;

while ( <FILE> )
{
    $i++;
    next unless /^[^\t]+(\t[^\t]+){4}$/;
    print $_;
}

close( FILE );
```

How It Works

Here's a walk-through of this expression:

^	the beginning of the line, followed by . . .
[^\t]	a character class that isn't a tab . . .
+	found one or many times . . .
(	a group that contains . . .
\t	a tab, followed by . . .
[^\t]	a character class that isn't a tab . . .
+	found one or many times . . .
)	the end of the group . . .
{4}	found four times, up to . . .
$	the end of the line.

PHP

```
<html>
<head><title>3-2 Finding bad tab-delimited records</title></head>
<body>
<form action="recipe3-2.php" method="post">
<textarea name="records" cols="20" rows="10"></textarea><br/>
<input type="submit" value="Find the bad records" /><br/><br/>
<?php
if ( $SERVER['REQUEST_METHOD'] == "POST" )
{
    $lines = explode( "\n", $_POST['records'] );
    foreach ($lines as $line)
    {
        if ( preg_match( "/^[^\t]+(\t[^\t]+){4}$/", $line ) )
        {
            print "<b>$line</b><br/>";
        }
    }
}
?>
</form>
</body>
</html>
```

How It Works

See "How It Works" under the Perl example in this recipe for an explanation of this expression.

Shell Scripting

```
$ grep '^[^    ]\+\(    [^    ]\+\)\{4\}$' filename
```

How It Works

The grep command doesn't work well with the \t character class inside [ ] on the command line, so the program uses a real tab. To insert a tab on the command line, press the Ctrl+V combination and then press the Tab key. The other modification you should be aware of is that (,), +, {, and } are escaped.

Vim

`/^[^\t]\+\(\t[^\t]\+\)\{4\}$`

How It Works

Look at the "How It Works" section under the Perl recipe to see how this expression operates. Remember that when using searches in Vim, escape the (,), +, {, and } characters.

3-3. Changing CSV Files to Tab-Delimited Files

This recipe shows you how to change CSV files to tab-delimited files, taking care to not replace commas that are inside quotes.

Perl

```
#!/usr/bin/perl -w
use strict;

open( FILE, $ARGV[0] ) || die "Cannot open file!";

my $i = 0;

while ( <FILE> )
{
    my $line = $_;
    $line =~ s/,(?=(?:[^"]*$)|(?:[^"]*"[^"]*"[^"]*)*$)/\t/go;
    print $line;
}

close( FILE );
```

How It Works

This expression will work only on valid CSV files. It works by assuming that only commas outside quotes should be replaced with tabs, and it accomplishes that task by making sure an even number of quotes appear *after* each comma or that no quotes appear after the comma at all.

This works even with escaped quotes in CSV files, because in CSV files the double quote is escaped by doubling it: "". This makes the expression for checking the even number of quotes a lot easier.

You may wonder why I didn't check to see if the number of quotes *before* each comma is even. This is only because of a limitation in Perl's regular expression interpreter—variable-length expressions aren't allowed in look-behinds. Therefore, you have to use a look-ahead that, in the end, accomplishes the same thing. After all, quotes appear in even numbers. If an odd number before a comma suggests it's in quotes, then an odd number after the comma also suggests it's in quotes.

Here's the expression, broken down at a high level:

,	a comma . . .
(?=	a positive look-ahead that contains . . .
(?:...)	a nonmatching group that contains the first expression . . .
|	or . . .
(?:...)	a noncapturing group that contains the second expression.

The first expression makes sure that no quotes appear between the comma and the end of the line.

[^   a character class that isn't . . .

"   a double quote . . .

]   the end of the character class . . .

*   found zero or more times . . .

$ the end of the line.

The second noncapturing group contains an expression to ensure that if a quote appears between the comma and the end of the line, then the comma isn't preceded by a quote and is followed by another one. This method ensures an even number of quotes appears between the comma and the end of the line.

[^   a character class that *doesn't* contain . . .

"   a double quote . . .

]   the end of the character class . . .

*   found zero or more times . . .

"   a quote, followed by . . .

[^   a character class that *doesn't* contain . . .

"   a quote . . .

]   the end of the character class . . .

*   found zero or more times . . .

"   a double quote . . .

[^   a character class that *doesn't* contain . . .

"   a quote . . .

]   the end of the character class . . .

*   found zero or more times . . .

)   the end of the group . . .

*   found zero or more times . . .

$ the end of the line.

PHP

```
<html>
<head><title>3-3 Changing CSV files to tab-delimited files</title></head>
<body>
<form action="recipe3-3.php" method="post">
<textarea name="records" cols="20" rows="10"></textarea><br/>
<input type="submit" value="CSV to tab" /><br/><br/>
<?php
if ( $_SERVER['REQUEST_METHOD'] == "POST" )
{
    $lines = explode( "\n", $_POST['records'] );
    foreach ($lines as $line)
    {
        $newstr = preg_replace( "/,(?=(?:[^"]*$)|(?:[^"]*"[^"]*"[^"]*)*$)/",
            "\t", $line );
        print "<b>$newstr</b><br/>";
    }
}
?>
</form>
</body>
</html>
```

How It Works

Read about how this expression works in the Perl section of this recipe.

Vim

```
:%s/,\(\%([^"]*$\)\|\%([^"]*"[^"]*"[^"]*\)*$\)\@=/\t/g
```

How It Works

The Vim expression checks to make sure the comma that's going to be replaced isn't in quotes. It does this by using a look-ahead to make sure an even number of quotes appears between the comma and the end of the line, if a quote is found at all.

,	a comma followed by ...
\(	a group that contains ...
\%(	a noncapturing group that contains ...
[^	a character class that *doesn't* contain ...
"	a quote ...
]	the end of the character class ...

*	found zero or more times . . .
$	the end of the line . . .
\)	the end of the group . . .
|	or . . .
\%(	a noncapturing group that contains . . .
[^	a character group that *doesn't* contain . . .
"	a quote . . .
]	the end of the character class . . .
*	found zero or more times . . .
"	a quote . . .
[^	a class that doesn't contain . . .
"	a quote . . .
]	the end of the character class . . .
*	zero or more times . . .
"	a quote . . .
[^	a class that doesn't contain . . .
"	a quote . . .
]	the end of the character class . . .
*	zero or more times . . .
\)	the end of the group . . .
*	found zero or more times . . .
$	the end of the line . . .
\)	the end of the group . . .
\)@=	the preceding expression is a look-ahead.

In this case, the preceding expression is everything after the comma.

3-4. Changing Tab-Delimited Files to CSV Files

This recipe allows you to change a tab-delimited file into a CSV file. Commas and quotes already in the fields are escaped.

Perl

```perl
#!/usr/bin/perl -w
use strict;

open( FILE, $ARGV[0] ) || die "Cannot open file!";

my $i = 0;

while ( <FILE> )
{
    my $line = $_;
    $line =~ s/\t(?=(?:[^\"]*$)|(?:[^\"]*\"[^\"]*\")*$)/,/go;
    print $line;
}

close( FILE );
```

How It Works

Here's the expression, broken down:

\t	a tab ...
(?=	a positive look-ahead that contains ...
(?:	a nonmatching group that contains ...
[^	a character class that isn't ...
\"	a double quote ...
]	the end of the character class ...
*	found zero or more times ...
$	the end of the line ...
)	the end of the group ...
		or ...
(?:	a noncapturing group that contains ...
[^	a character class that *doesn't* contain ...
\"	a double quote ...

]	the end of the character class . . .
*	found zero or more times . . .
\"	a quote, followed by . . .
[^	a character class that *doesn't* contain . . .
\"	a quote . . .
]	the end of the character class . . .
*	found zero or more times . . .
\"	a double quote . . .
)	the end of the group . . .
*	found zero or more times . . .
$	the end of the line . . .
)	the end of the group.

PHP

```
<html>
<head><title>3-4 Changing tab-delimited files to CSV files</title></head>
<body>
<form action="recipe3-4.php" method="post">
<textarea name="records" cols="20" rows="10"></textarea><br/>
<input type="submit" value="Tab to CSV" /><br/><br/>
<?php
if ( $_SERVER['REQUEST_METHOD'] == "POST" )
{
    $lines = explode( "\n", $_POST['records'] );
    foreach ($lines as $line)
    {
        $newstr = preg_replace( "/\t(?=(?:[^\"]*$)|(?:[^\"]*\"[^\"]*\")*$)/",
",", $line );
        print "<b>$newstr</b><br/>";
    }
}
?>
</form>
</body>
</html>
```

How It Works

See "How It Works" under the Perl example for this expression to see it broken down.

Vim

`:%s/\t\(\%([^"]*$\)\|\%([^"]*"[^"]*"\)*$\)\@=/,/g`

How It Works

The Vim expression checks to make sure each tab that's going to be replaced isn't in quotes. Here's the Vim expression, broken down:

\t	a comma followed by . . .
\(	a group that contains . . .
\%(	a noncapturing group that contains . . .
[^	a character class that *doesn't* contain . . .
"	a quote . . .
]	the end of the character class . . .
*	found zero or more times . . .
$	the end of the line . . .
\)	the end of the group . . .
|	or . . .
\%(	a noncapturing group that contains . . .
[^	a character group that *doesn't* contain . . .
"	a quote . . .
]	the end of the character class . . .
*	found zero or more times . . .
"	a quote . . .
[^	a class that *doesn't* contain . . .
"	a quote . . .
]	the end of the character class . . .
*	zero or more times . . .
"	a quote . . .
\)	the end of the group . . .

*	found zero or more times . . .
$	the end of the line . . .
\)	the end of the group . . .
\)@=	the preceding expression is a look-ahead.

In this case, the preceding expression is everything after the tab.

3-5. Extracting CSV Fields

This recipe shows you how to extract a particular field from a correctly formatted CSV file. In this recipe, let's assume it's the second field in each line that you want to extract.

Perl

```
#!/usr/bin/perl -w
use strict;

open( FILE, $ARGV[0] ) || die "Cannot open file!";

my $i = 0;

while ( <FILE> )
{
    my $field = $_;
    $field =~ s/^(?:[^",]+|"(?:[^"]|\\")*"),([^",]+|"(?:[^"]|\\")*")↵
(?:,.*)$/$1/;
    print $field;
}

close( FILE );
```

How It Works

This expression uses noncapturing parentheses, which are set off by (?:, to ignore parts of the CSV record that are unimportant to the replacement. Since the expression for a single CSV field is explained in detail in recipe 3-1, the following is a high-level overview of the expression:

^	the beginning of the line . . .
(?:...)	a single CSV field, followed by . . .
,	a comma, then . . .
(...)	a capturing CSV field, followed by . . .
(?:	a noncapturing group that contains . . .
,	a comma and . . .
.	any character . . .
*	found none, one, or many times, up to . . .
)	the end of the group . . .
$	the end of the line.

The CSV field expression is `(?:[^",]+|"(?:[^"]|\\")*")`, which doesn't actually capture any text. The second expression is nearly the same but is `([^",]+|"(?:[^"]|\\")*")`. Note that the only difference is the beginning parenthesis.

PHP

```
<html>
<head><title>3-5 Extracting CSV fields</title></head>
<body>
<form action="recipe3-5.php" method="post">
<textarea name="records" cols="20" rows="10"></textarea><br/>
<input type="submit" value="Show me field 2" /><br/><br/>
<?php
if ( $_SERVER['REQUEST_METHOD'] == "POST" )
{
    $lines = explode( "\n", $_POST['records'] );
    foreach ($lines as $line)
    {
        $field = preg_replace(
"/^(?:[^\",]+|\"(?:[^\"]|\\\")*\"),([^\",]+|\"(?:[^\"]|\\\")*\")(?:,.*)$/",
"$1", $line );
        print "<b>$field</b><br/>";
    }
}
?>
</form>
</body>
</html>
```

How It Works

The PHP recipe shown here takes the lines in the text box and parses them. The second field is printed to the form after it's submitted.

See "How It Works" under the Perl section of this recipe for an explanation of the expression. The PHP expression requires double quotes to be escaped, but other than that the expressions are identical.

CSV AND TAB-DELIMITED FILES

3-6. Extracting Tab-Delimited Fields

You can use this recipe to print a single field from a correctly formatted tab-delimited record. For the sake of this example, field two will be extracted from each record in a file or set of lines.

Perl

```perl
#!/usr/bin/perl -w
use strict;

open( FILE, $ARGV[0] ) || die "Cannot open file!";

my $i = 0;

while ( <FILE> )
{
    my $field = $_;
    $field =~ s/^(?:[^\t]+\t)([^\t]+)(?:\t.*)$/$1/;
    print $field;
}

close( FILE );
```

How It Works

This expression uses a smaller expression, ([^\t]+), to say "anything that isn't a tab," which defines a tab-delimited field. Some changes are modifying the groups with (?: to make them noncapturing groups so that there's no confusion about what will be included in the back reference.

The expression breaks down as follows:

^   the beginning of the line, followed by a . . .

(?:   a noncapturing group that includes . . .

[^\t]   a character class that isn't a tab . . .

+   found one or more times, up to . . .

\t   a tab, then . . .

)   the end of the group . . .

(a capturing group that includes . . .

[^\t]   a character class that isn't a tab . . .

+   one or more times, followed by . . .

)   the end of the group . . .

(?:   a noncapturing group . . .

\t	a tab ...
.	any character ...
*	zero, one, or many times, up to ...
)	the end of the group ...
$	the end of the line.

PHP

```
<html>
<head><title>3-6 Extracting tab-delimited fields</title></head>
<body>
<form action="recipe3-6.php" method="post">
<textarea name="records" cols="20" rows="10"></textarea><br/>
<input type="submit" value="Show me field 2" /><br/><br/>
<?php
if ( $_SERVER['REQUEST_METHOD'] == "POST" )
{
    $lines = explode( "\n", $_POST['records'] );
    foreach ($lines as $line)
    {
        $field = preg_replace( "/^(?:[^\t]+\t)([^\t]+)(?:\t.*)$/",
            "$1", $line );
        print "<b>$field</b><br/>";
    }
}
?>
</form>
</body>
</html>
```

CSV AND TAB-DELIMITED FILES

How It Works

The PHP recipe takes multiple lines from a text area, splits them into an array based on the newline character ("\n"), and iterates through each element in the array to make replacements. The replacement in this case is whatever was found in the second tab-delimited field, as found by the capturing group in the expression.

To see more about how the expression works, refer to "How It Works" under the Perl section of this recipe.

CHAPTER 4

■■■

Formatting and Validating

The recipes in this chapter focus on formatting and validating text. They're particularly useful in validation routines in applications, where user input can vary but must conform to basic rules. U.S. postal codes are an example of this—some applications may require all nine digits, and some may allow all nine but just require five, as in the case of 55555-0000 or 55555, respectively.

4-1. Formatting U.S. Phone Numbers

You can use this recipe to format a string of numbers, such as 3334445555 into (333) 444-5555. The regular expressions will allow you to do the work without using substrings and finding positions of characters within the string. The recipe will also format the phone number into the new format if it looks like 333.444.5555 and 333-444-5555.

Perl

```
#!/usr/bin/perl -w
use strict;

my $phonenumber = $ARGV[0];

$phonenumber =~ s/^\(?(\d{3})\)?[- .]?(\d{3})[- .]?(\d{4})$/($1) $2-$3/;
print "'" . $phonenumber . "'\n";
```

How It Works

This recipe captures three groups of digits and uses them in the replacement expression. The character class \d is used instead of [0-9], which makes it a little more concise.

^	the beginning of the line . . .
\(	a literal parenthesis . . .
?	found zero or one time . . .
(	a capturing group containing . . .
\d	a digit . . .
{3}	found three times . . .
)	the end of the group . . .
\)	up to a literal parenthesis . . .
[- .]	a character class that matches a hyphen (-), a space ( ), or a dot (.) . . .
?	found at most once . . .
. . .	the rest of the expression.

The rest of the expression is essentially a repeat of the previous, with a few modifications. A literal (and) may appear around the first group of three digits.

The character class [- .] matches a hyphen, space, or dot (period). The ? after the class makes it optional, which is why the expression also matches numbers that run together. Note the hyphen (-) is first in the character class—this is important if the hyphen is to be taken literally and not used to define a range within the character class.

PHP

```
<html>
<head><title>4-1 Formatting phone numbers</title></head>
<body>
<form action="recipe4-1.php" method="post">
<input type="text" name="phonenumber" /><br/>
<input type="submit" value="Format my number" /><br/><br/>
<?php
if ( $_SERVER['REQUEST_METHOD'] == "POST" )
{
    $phonenumber = $_POST['phonenumber'];
    $newnumber = preg_replace( "/^\(?(\d{3})\)?[- .]?(\d{3})[- .]?(\d{4})$/",
        "($1) $2-$3", $phonenumber );
    print "<b>'$newnumber'</b><br/>";
}
?>
</form>
</body>
</html>
```

How It Works

This recipe uses Perl-Compatible Regular Expressions (PCREs) provided by preg_replace(), so you can learn more about how it works under the "How It Works" section under the Perl recipe.

Vim

```
%s/^(\?\(\d\{3}\))\)\?[- .]\?\(\d\{3}\)[- .]\?\(\d\{4}\)/(\1) \2-\3/g
```

How It Works

The Vim expression is quite long, but it's made up mostly of escape characters (\) that are giving (,), ?, and { their special meaning. If you take out all the \ characters, you can follow the expression using the "How It Works" explanation under the Perl example in this recipe.

■ **See Also** 4-2, 4-3, 4-5, 4-6, 4-8, 4-13, 4-14, 4-15, 4-16, 4-18, 4-20, 6-10, 6-18, 6-20, 6-21

FORMATTING AND VALIDATING

4-2. Formatting U.S. Dates

This recipe demonstrates changing different date formats into one format. This recipe will change 3/1/2004 or 3.1.2004 into 3-1-2004.

Perl

```
#!/usr/bin/perl -w
use strict;

my $date = $ARGV[0] || die "Please supply a parameter!";

$date =~ s/^(\d{1,2})[-\/.]?(\d{1,2})[-\/.]?((?:\d{2}|\d{4}))$/$1-$2-$3/;
print "'" . $date . "'\n";
```

How It Works

This recipe uses the \d character class as a shortcut to refer to [0-9]. It groups the numbers in the original string and uses back references to replace the string with a reformatted version. The following is the expression broken down into parts:

^	the beginning of the line . . .
(	a capturing group . . .
\d	a digit . . .
{1,2}	found one to two times . . .
)	the end of the group . . .
[-\/.]	a character class that can include a dash, a slash, or a dot . . .
?	found at most one time . . .
...	this group repeats for the DD part of the date . . .
(	a group that contains . . .
(?:	a noncapturing group that can contain . . .
\d	a digit . . .
{2}	found two times . . .
|	for . . .
\d	a digit . . .

{4}   found four times . . .

)   the end of the group . . .

)   the end of the outer group . . .

$ the end of the line.

The escape before the slash (\/) isn't required for the expression—it's required for Perl because I'm using / as a delimiter. I describe this in greater detail in the "Syntax Overview" section earlier in this book.

■Note This expression will find some strings ambiguous. For instance, 12303 will yield 12-3-03, but the user may mean 1-23-03.

PHP

```
<html>
<head><title>4-2 Formatting US Dates</title></head>
<body>
<form action="recipe4-2.php" method="post">
<input type="text" name="date" /><br/>
<input type="submit" value="Format my date" /><br/><br/>
<?php
if ( $_SERVER['REQUEST_METHOD'] == "POST" )
{
    $date = $_POST['date'];
    $newdate = preg_replace( "/^(\d{1,2})[-\/.]?(\d{1,2})↵
[-\/.]?((?:\d{2}|\d{4}))$/", "$1-$2-$3", $date );
    print "<b>'$newdate'</b><br/>";
}
?>
</form>
</body>
</html>
```

How It Works

See "How It Works" under the Perl example of this recipe for details about how this expression operates.

Vim

`%s/^\(\d\{1,2}\)[-\/.]\?\(\d\{1,2}\)[-\/.]\?\(\(\d\{2}\|\d\{4}\)\)\)$/\1-\2-\3/g`

How It Works

To walk through the expression, see "How It Works" under the Perl example in this recipe. Remember that in Vim, \(, \?, and \{ have special meanings and are literal when they aren't escaped, which is the opposite of PCRE.

■**See Also** 4-1, 4-3, 4-5, 4-6, 4-8, 4-13, 4-14, 4-15, 4-16, 4-18, 4-20, 6-10, 6-18, 6-20, 6-21

4-3. Validating Alternate Dates

This expression validates dates in a different format than the ones in recipe 4-2. Matches for this are as follows:

```
20-Jul-2004
1-Oct-1999
```

It's even smart enough to match months with the correct number of days, but it won't check to see if the leap year is correct. In this recipe, the case is important—see the "Variations" section at the end of this recipe for hints on making the matches case insensitive.

Perl

```perl
#!/usr/bin/perl -w
use strict;

my $date = $ARGV[0] || die "What!?!";

if ( $date =~ /^(?:(?:(?:0[1-9]|[12][0-9]|30)-(?:Sep|Apr|Jun|Nov))| ⏎
(?:(?:0[1-9]|[12][0-9])-Feb)|(?:(?:0[1-9]|[12][0-9]|3[01])- ⏎
(?:Jan|Mar|May|Jul|Aug|Oct|Dec)))-\d{4}$/ ) {
    print "Found valid date:   " . $date . "\n";
} else {
    print "Found invalid date:   " . $date . "\n";
}

exit 0;
```

How It Works

The bulk of this expression consists of ranges that validate the number of days in each month. For brevity, I'll break down the first range set that validates the months of the year that have only 30 days. ("Thirty days has September, April, June, and November . . ..")

The i modifier used in the expression makes sure that the expression is case insensitive, so using all capital letters will work.

The expression itself breaks down into the following:

(?:	a noncapturing group that contains . . .
(?:	another noncapturing group with . . .
0	zero, followed by . . .
[	a character class with . . .
1-9	one through nine . . .
]	the end of the character class . . .

	or . . .
[	a character class with . . .
12	a one or a two . . .
]	the end of the character class . . .
[	a character class including . . .
0-9	zero through nine . . .
]	the end of the character class . . .
|	or . . .
3	three, followed by . . .
0	zero . . .
)	the end of the group . . .
-	a dash . . .
(?:	a noncapturing group containing . . .
Sep	an S, e, p . . .
|	or . . .
Apr	an A, p, r . . .
|	or . . .
Jun	a J, u, n . . .
|	or . . .
Nov	an N, o, v . . .
)	the end of the group containing the month abbreviations . . .
)	the end of the group.

This just continues for each of the other possible combinations. The second large group, `(?:(?:0[1-9]|[12][0-9])-Feb)`, makes sure February has at most 29 days, but it won't check for leap years. The last expression will check for 31 days in the remaining 7 months.

PHP

```
<html>
<head><title>4-3 Validating Alternate Dates</title></head>
<body>
<form action="recipe4-3.php" method="post">
<input type="text" name="value" value="<? $_POST['value'] ?>" /><br/>
```

```php
<input type="submit" value="Validate date" /><br/><br/>
<?php
if ( $_SERVER['REQUEST_METHOD'] == "POST" )
{
    $str = $_POST['value'];

    if ( preg_match( "/^(?:(?:(?:0[1-9]|[12][0-9]|30)-(?:Sep|Apr|Jun|Nov))| ⏎
(?:(?:0[1-9]|[12][0-9])-Feb)|(?:(?:0[1-9]|[12][0-9]|3[01])- ⏎
(?:Jan|Mar|May|Jul|Aug|Oct|Nov|Dec)))-\d{4}$/",  $str ) )
    {
        print "<b>Found valid date: " . $str . "</b><br/>";
    }
    else
    {
        print "<b>Found invalid date: " . $str . "</b><br/>";
    }
}
?>
</form>
</body>
</html>
```

How It Works

See "How It Works" under the Perl example in this recipe.

Shell Scripting

```
$ grep '^\(\(\(0[1-9]\|[12][0-9]\|30\)-\(Sep\|Apr\|Jun\|Nov\)\)\| ⏎
\(\(0[1-9]\|[12]\[0-9]\)-Feb\)\|\(\(0[1-9]\|[12][0-9]\|3[01]\)- ⏎
\(Jan\|Mar\|May\|Jul\|Aug\|Oct\|Nov\|Dec\)\)\)-[0-9]\{4\}$' filename
```

How It Works

I know what you're thinking: "This isn't any easier than using code!" It's really not as bad as it looks. Just walk through the expression under the Perl example, and remember to escape (,), |, {, and }.

Vim

```
/^\(\(\(0[1-9]\|[12][0-9]\|30\)-\(Sep\|Apr\|Jun\|Nov\)\)\| ⏎
\(\(0[1-9]\|[12]\[0-9]\)-Feb\)\|\(\(0[1-9]\|[12][0-9]\|3[01]\)- ⏎
\(Jan\|Mar\|May\|Jul\|Aug\|Oct\|Nov\|Dec\)\)\)-[0-9]\{4\}$
```

How It Works

See "How It Works" under the Perl example in this recipe. Remember to escape (,), |, {, and }.

Note You may get what looks like an error from Vim when you try to use this expression. It says, "Press ENTER or type command to continue." This is just the behavior of Vim. Just type **enter**, and the search will continue.

Variations

You can modify this recipe slightly to catch the months if they're in all uppercase or lowercase.

For Perl and PHP, use the i option with the search functions. Use the -i parameter with grep, and in Vim add the \c sequence somewhere in the expression to make the search case insensitive.

See the "Syntax Overview" section in this book for more information on each language.

See Also 2-1, 2-15, 4-10, 4-14, 4-16, 4-17

4-4. Formatting Large Numbers

This recipe adds commas to large numbers to make them more readable. A number such as 383894012 becomes 383,894,012. This recipe operates on whole numbers and assumes no decimal point appears in the number.

Perl

```perl
#!/usr/bin/perl -w
use strict;

my $largenumber = $ARGV[0] || die "Supply a parameter!";

$largenumber =~ s/(?<=\d)(?=(\d{3})+(?!\d))/,/g;
print "'" . $largenumber . "'\n";
```

How It Works

This recipe consists entirely of look-aheads and look-behinds. The following is the expression broken down into parts:

`(?<=`	a positive look-behind including . . .
`\d`	a number . . .
`)`	the end of the positive look-behind . . .
`(?=`	a positive look-ahead including . . .
`(`	a group that contains . . .
`\d`	a number . . .
`{3}`	found three times . . .
`)`	the end of the group . . .
`+`	found one or more times . . .
`(?!`	a negative look-ahead that contains . . .
`\d`	a number . . .
`)`	the end of the negative look-ahead . . .
`)`	the end of the positive look-ahead.

The position where the comma is inserted is between the look-behind and look-ahead. The look-ahead groups numbers in threes where a number doesn't appear afterward (that could be the end of the line, a decimal point, or a label such as Kb).

PHP

```
<html>
<head><title>4-4 Formatting large numbers</title></head>
<body>
<form action="recipe4-4.php" method="post">
<input type="text" name="lnumber" /><br/>
<input type="submit" value="Add commas" /><br/><br/>
<?php
if ( $_SERVER['REQUEST_METHOD'] == "POST" )
{
    $lnumber = $_POST['lnumber'];
    $newlnumber = preg_replace( "/(?<=\d)(?=(\d{3})+(?!\d))/", ",", $lnumber );
    print "<b>'$newlnumber'</b><br/>";
}
?>
</form>
</body>
</html>
```

How It Works

This recipe uses PCRE, so you can follow the "How It Works" section under the Perl example.

Vim

```
%s/\d\@<=\(\(\d\{3}\)\)\+\d\@!\)\@=/,/g
```

How It Works

This expression is much easier to follow if you keep in mind that \@= is the same as (?= in Perl, except Vim look-aheads and look-behinds appear *after* the expression they modify. The following is how the Vim expression breaks down:

\d	a number ...
\@<=	that's found before ...
\(	a group that contains ...
\(	another group with ...
\d	a number ...
\{3}	three times ...
\)	the end of the group ...
\+	that's found at least once, where ...

\d   a digit . . .

\@!   that isn't found ahead . . .

\)   the end of the group . . .

\@=   defines this group as a look-ahead.

See Also 4-4, 5-1, 5-2, 5-3, 5-4

4-5. Formatting Negative Numbers

This recipe will identify negative numbers, such as -34.44, and wrap them in parentheses to get (34.44).

Perl

```
#!/usr/bin/perl -w
use strict;

my $negativenumber = $ARGV[0];

$negativenumber =~ s/^-([\d.,]+)$/($1)/;
print "'" . $negativenumber . "'\n";
```

How It Works

This expression captures numbers that are preceded by a negative sign, and it surrounds the numbers with parentheses. Here's the expression broken down:

^	the beginning of the line . . .
-	a negative sign . . .
(	a capturing group . . .
[\d.,]	a character class that includes a number, a decimal point, or a comma . . .
)	the end of the capturing group . . .
+	found one for more times . . .
$	the end of the line.

PHP

```
<html>
<head><title>4-5 Formatting negative numbers</title></head>
<body>
<form action="recipe4-5.php" method="post">
<input type="text" name="negnumber" /><br/>
<input type="submit" value="Format number" /><br/><br/>
<?php
if ( $_SERVER['REQUEST_METHOD'] == "POST" )
{
        $negnumber = $_POST['negnumber'];
        $newnegnumber = preg_replace( "/^-([\d.,]+)$/", "($1)", $negnumber );
        print "<b>'$newnegnumber'</b><br/>";
```

```
}
?>
</form>
</body>
</html>
```

How It Works

Look at "How It Works" under the Perl example of this recipe for a breakdown of this expression.

Vim

```
%s/^-\(\(\d\|.\|,\)\+\)$/(\1)/g
```

How It Works

You can break the Vim expression down like this:

^	the beginning of the line . . .
-	a dash . . .
\(	a group that contains . . .
\(	another group with . . .
\d	a number . . .
|	or . . .
.	a decimal point . . .
|	or . . .
,	a comma . . .
\)	the end of the group . . .
\+	found one or more times . . .
\)	the end of the outermost group . . .
$	the end of the line.

The group captured by the outside \(and \) will be inserted by the back reference \1 in the replacement expression.

4-6. Formatting Single Digits

This expression adds a zero to the beginning of a number that's a single digit, such as a number less than ten. An example is 3/4/2004, which will be reprinted as 03/04/2004.

Perl

```
#!/usr/bin/perl -w
use strict;
my $digit = $ARGV[0] || die "No, no, no.  I came here for an argument.";
$digit =~ s/(?:(?<=^)|(?<=[^\d]))(\d)(?=[^\d])/0$1/g;
print "'" . $digit . "'\n";
```

How It Works

This expression uses look-behinds and look-aheads to take notice of what's located around the single digit. It then uses a back reference to add a zero to the beginning of the digit. The following is a breakdown of the group that looks behind the digit:

(?:	a noncapturing group that contains . . .
(?<=	a positive look-behind that contains . . .
^	the beginning of the line . . .
)	the end of the positive look-behind . . .
|	for . . .
(?<=	another positive look-behind that contains . . .
[^\d]	a character class that isn't a digit . . .
)	the end of the positive look-behind . . .
)	the end of the noncapturing group.

The digit is captured by (\d), which is then followed by a look-ahead group that simply looks for a nondigit matched by the character class [^\d].

PHP

```
<html>
<head><title>4-6 Formatting single digits</title></head>
<body>
<form action="recipe4-6.php" method="post">
<input type="text" name="digit" /><br/>
<input type="submit" value="Format number" /><br/><br/>
<?php
if ( $_SERVER['REQUEST_METHOD'] == "POST" )
```

```
{
    $digit = $_POST['digit'];
    $newdigit = preg_replace( "/(?:(?<=^)|(?<=[^\d]))(\d)(?=[^\d])/",
        "0$1", $digit );
    print "<b>'$newdigit'</b><br/>";
}
?>
</form>
</body>
</html>
```

How It Works

Refer to "How It Works" under the Perl example of this recipe to see how this expression works.

See Also 4-4, 5-1, 5-2, 5-3, 5-4

4-7. Limiting User Input to Alpha Characters

This simple recipe allows you to make sure user input is limited to characters in the alphabet.

Perl

```perl
#!/usr/bin/perl -w
use strict;

my $input = $ARGV[0];

if ( $input =~ /^[a-z]+$/i )
{
        print "Thanks for the input:  '" . $input . "'\n";
} else {
        print "Alpha only, please!\n";
}
```

How It Works

This expression uses a character class and the range operator - to create a range from a to z, with the i flag used to capture uppercase:

^	the beginning of the line . . .
[a-z]	the character class containing a range from *a* to *z* . . .
+	found one or more times, until . . .
$	the end of the line.

PHP

```php
<html>
<head><title>4-7 Limiting user input to alpha characters</title></head>
<style>
    .err { color : red ; font-weight : bold }
</style>
<body>
<form action="recipe4-7.php" method="post">
<input type="text" name="input" /><br/>
<input type="submit" value="Submit Form" /><br/><br/>
<?php
if ( preg_match( "/^[a-z]+$/i", $input ) )
{
    $input = $_POST['input'];
    if ( preg_match( "/^[a-z]+$/i", $input ) )
    {
```

```
            # Do some processing here - input if valid
        }
        else
        {
            print "<span class=\"err\">Alpha only.  Please correct and " .
                "resubmit the form</span><br/>";
        }
}
?>
</form>
</body>
</html>
```

How It Works

This PHP example uses the expression as a method of controlling flow. You can check to make sure the input is valid before doing more processing. If the input isn't valid, the form is redrawn with an error message.

I explain the expression in detail under the "How It Works" section in the Perl example.

Shell Scripting

```
$ grep -i '^[a-z]+$' filename
```

How It Works

See "How It Works" under the Perl example of this recipe for a closer look at this expression.

Vim

```
/^[A-Za-z]\+$
```

How It Works

You can use this expression in Vim to find lines that have only characters from the alphabet in them, from beginning to end. The expression adds the escape character \ before the + qualifier to make it one character different from the PCRE expressions.

See Also 2-11, 2-12, 2-13, 2-14, 4-11, 4-12, 4-21, 6-18

FORMATTING AND VALIDATING

4-8. Validating U.S. Currency

This simple recipe validates U.S. currency. It checks for the existence of a dollar sign at the beginning, allows any number of digits, and requires a decimal point with two numbers after it. Valid matches are $1000.00, $34.83, and $343.33.

Perl

```perl
#!/usr/bin/perl -w
use strict;

my $input = $ARGV[0] || die "Parameter required.";

if ( $input =~  /^\$\d+\.\d\d$/ )
{
        print "Thanks for the input:  '" . $input . "'\n";
} else {
        print "How much?\n";
}
```

How It Works

The expression, broken down, is as follows:

^	the beginning of the line . . .
\$	a literal $ . . .
\d	a digit . . .
+	one or more times . . .
\.	a decimal point . . .
\d	a number . . .
\d	another number . . .
$	the end of the line.

PHP

```php
<html>
<head><title>4-8 Validating U.S. currency</title></head>
<style>
    .err { color : red ; font-weight : bold }
</style>
<body>
<form action="recipe4-8.php" method="post">
<input type="text" name="input" /><br/>
```

```
<input type="submit" value="Submit Form" /><br/><br/>
<?php
if ( $_SERVER['REQUEST_METHOD'] == "POST" )
{
    $input = $_POST['input'];
    if ( preg_match( "/^[$]\d+\.\d\d$/", $input ) )
    {
        # Do some processing here - input if valid
    }
    else
    {
        print "<span class=\"err\">Invalid amount.</span><br/>";
    }
}
?>
</form>
</body>
</html>
```

How It Works

This is one of the few times when the PCRE expression supported by preg_match() is different from the Perl expression. The difference here is how the literal $ is treated; in this expression the $ is wrapped in a character class [$]. I cover the rest of the expression in the "How It Works" section in the Perl example.

Shell Scripting

```
$ grep -E '^\$[0-9]+\.[0-9][0-9]$' filename
```

How It Works

The \d character class isn't supported by Portable Operating System Interface (POSIX) extended, so this recipe uses the character class [0-9] instead. The expression broken down is as follows:

^	the beginning of the line . . .
\$	a literal dollar sign . . .
[0-9]	any number zero through nine . . .
+	found one or more times . . .
\.	a literal dot or decimal point . . .
[0-9]	any number zero through nine . . .
[0-9]	again . . .
$	the end of the line.

Vim

```
/^\$\d\+.\d\d$
```

How It Works

The previous expression is like the expressions in the Perl and PHP examples, with the exception of the escaped plus \+. For more information about this expression, see "How It Works" under the Perl example.

See Also 4-1, 4-2, 4-3, 4-4, 4-5, 4-13, 4-14, 4-15, 4-16, 4-18, 4-20, 6-10, 6-18, 6-20, 6-21

FORMATTING AND VALIDATING

4-9. Limiting User Input to 15 Characters

This expression highlights the technique of using ranges in qualifiers to limit user input to 15 characters. You can modify the expression to allow any minimum or maximum string length.

Perl

```
#!/usr/bin/perl -w
use strict;
my $input = $ARGV[0];

if ( $input =~ /^.{0,15}$/ )
{
    print "Input '" . $input . "' is valid\n";
} else {
    print "No more than 15 characters!\n";
}
```

How It Works

The expression says quite simply the following:

^	the beginning of the line . . .
.	any character . . .
{0,15}	found 0 through 15 times . . .
$	the end of the line.

PHP

```
<html>
<head><title>4-9 Limiting user input to 15 characters</title></head>
<style>
    .err { color : red ; font-weight : bold }
</style>
<body>
<form action="recipe4-9.php" method="post">
<input type="text" name="input" /><br/>
<input type="submit" value="Submit Form" /><br/><br/>
<?php
if ( $_SERVER['REQUEST_METHOD'] == "POST" )
{
    $input = $_POST['input'];
    if ( preg_match( "/^.{0,15}$/", $input ) )
    {
        # Do some processing here - input if valid
```

```
        }
        else
        {
            print "<span class=\"err\">Input too long.  Please " .
                "correct and resubmit the form</span><br/>";
        }
    }
    ?>
    </form>
    </body>
    </html>
```

How It Works

When this form is posted to itself, it evaluates the input using the PCRE provided by preg_match(). If the value doesn't match the expression, the page prints a message to the screen.

I explain the expression shown in further detail under "How It Works" in the Perl example of this recipe.

Shell Scripting

```
$ grep -E '^.{0,15}$' filename
```

How It Works

To see how this expression works, refer to "How It Works" under the Perl example in this recipe.

Vim

```
/^.\{0,15}$
```

How It Works

You can use this expression to search for lines with 0 through 15 characters in them. For more about how this expression works, see the Perl example in this recipe, but make sure to add the escape before the range, like so: \{0,15}.

See Also 1-9, 2-8, 2-13, 2-14, 4-2, 4-11, 4-20

4-10. Validating IP Addresses

You can use this recipe to validate an IP address as four groups of numbers between 0 and 255 separated by periods. The address 192.168.0.1 is valid, but 256.0.1.2 isn't.

Perl

```
#!/usr/bin/perl -w
use strict;

my $input = $ARGV[0];

if ( $input =~  /^(([1-9]?[0-9]|1[0-9]{2}|2[0-4][0-9]|25[0-5]).){3}↵
([1-9]?[0-9]|1[0-9]{2}|2[0-4][0-9]|25[0-5])$/ )
{
    print "IP '" . $input . "' is valid\n";
} else {
    print "Please enter a valid IP address!\n";
}
```

How It Works

The bulk of this expression is a group that breaks down the numbers that range from 0 to 255. The expression would be a lot shorter if 002 or 015 were valid instead of 2 and 15, respectively, but for this expression you want to specify IP addresses without the leading zeros.

The range from 0 to 255 breaks down into other ranges: 0–99, 100–199, 200–249, and 250–255. The expression to match this is ([1-9]?[0-9]|1[0-9]{2}|2[0-4][0-9]|25[0-5]), which can be broken down into [1-9]?[0-9], which will match 0–99; 1[0-9]{2}, which will match 100–199; 2[0-4][0-9], which will match 200–249; and 25[0-5], which will match 250–255.

After taking out the IP address validation expression, the rest of it breaks down like this:

^   the beginning of the line . . .

(the beginning of a group that contains . . .

(...)   the IP address expression explained previously . . .

\.   a literal dot . . .

)   the end of the group . . .

{3}   occurring exactly three times . . .

(...)   another occurrence of the IP address . . .

$ the end of the line.

PHP

```
<html>
<head><title>4-10 Validating IP addresses</title></head>
<style>
        .err { color : red ; font-weight : bold }
</style>
<body>
<form action="recipe4-10.php" method="post">
<input type="text" name="input" /><br/>
<input type="submit" value="Submit Form" /><br/><br/>
<?php
if ( $_SERVER['REQUEST_METHOD'] == "POST" )
{
    $input = $_POST['input'];
    if ( preg_match( "/^(([1-9]?[0-9]|1[0-9]{2}|2[0-4][0-9]|25[0-5]).){3}↵
([1-9]?[0-9]|1[0-9]{2}|2[0-4][0-9]|25[0-5])$/", $input ) )
    {
        # Do some processing here - input if valid
    }
    else
    {
        print "<span class=\"err\">Bad IP address.  Please correct and " .
            "resubmit the form</span><br/>";
    }
}
?>
</form>
</body>
</html>
```

How It Works

Refer to "How It Works" under the Perl example under this recipe to see how the expression shown here works.

Shell Scripting

```
$ grep '^\(\([1-9]\?[0-9]\|1[0-9]\{2\}\|2[0-4][0-9]\|25[0-5]\)\.\)\{3\}↵
\([1-9]\?[0-9]\|1[0-9]\{2\}\|2[0-4][0-9]\|25[0-5]\)$' filename
```

How It Works

The expression shown previously, explained in greater detail under the Perl example, will allow you to view all lines in a file that contain valid IP addresses.

Vim

```
/^\(\([1-9]\?[0-9]\|1[0-9]\{2}\|2[0-4][0-9]\|25[0-5]\)\.\)\{3}\([1-9]\?↵
[0-9]\|1[0-9]\{2}\|2[0-4][0-9]\|25[0-5]\)$
```

How It Works

Aside from plenty of added escapes in this expression, it follows the expression used in the Perl example.

▧**See Also** 2-15

4-11. Validating E-mail Addresses

This recipe checks to make sure an e-mail address looks like a valid address, containing a username, @, and valid hostname. For example, null@example.com is valid, but NOSPAM@spam isn't valid.

Perl

```
#!/usr/bin/perl -w
use strict;

my $input = $ARGV[0];

if ( $input =~  /^[-\w.]+@([a-z0-9][-a-z0-9]+\.)+[a-z]{2,4}$/i )
{
        print "Email address '" . $input . "' is valid\n";
} else {
        print "Please enter a valid e-mail address!\n";
}
```

How It Works

The @ in the expression separates two different parts that match a username and a hostname. The expression to match the username is [-\w.]+, which matches a hyphen, a word character, or a dot one or more times.

The second expression, which matches the hostname, is a little more involved and breaks down as follows:

(	a group that includes . . .
[a-z0-9]	a letter or number . . .
[-a-z0-9]	a letter, number, or hyphen . . .
\.	a literal dot or period . . .
)	the end of the group . . .
+	found one or more times . . .
[a-z]	a letter . . .
{2,4}	found between two and four times.

This expression is based on the requirement that a label in a domain name can start with a letter or number but can't start with a hyphen. After the first character in the label, hyphens may appear. Labels are separated by dots where more than one of them is found in the expressions. This expression will match do-main.com but won't match -domain.com.

PHP

```
<html>
<head><title>4-11 Validating e-mail addresses</title></head>
<style>
    .err { color : red ; font-weight : bold }
</style>
<body>
<form action="recipe4-11.php" method="post">
<input type="text" name="input" /><br/>
<input type="submit" value="Submit Form" /><br/><br/>
<?php
if ( $_SERVER['REQUEST_METHOD'] == "POST" )
{
    $input = $_POST['input'];
    if ( preg_match( "/^[-\w.]+@([a-z0-9][-a-z0-9]+\.)+[a-z]{2,4}$/i",
$input ) )
    {
        # Do some processing here - input if valid
    }
    else
    {
        print "<span class=\"err\">Bad e-mail address.  Please correct ".
            "and resubmit the form</span><br/>";
    }
}
?>
</form>
</body>
</html>
```

How It Works

To read more about how this expression works, see "How It Works" under the Perl example of this recipe.

Shell Scripting

```
$ grep -E -1'^[-a-z0-9_.]+@([a-z0-9][-a-z0-9]+\.)+[a-z]{2,4}$' filename
```

How It Works

POSIX-extended expressions don't support the \w character class, so I've replaced \w with the longer but still functional [a-z0-9_]. The rest of the expression remains the same as the PCRE expressions given in the Perl and PHP examples.

FORMATTING AND VALIDATING

Vim

`/^[-A-Za-z0-9_.]\+@\([A-Za-z0-9][-A-Za-z0-9]\+\.\)\+[A-Za-z]\{2,4}$`

How It Works

In this example, you take the Perl or PHP expressions and add \ before any (, +, and { that you run across to get a valid Vim expression. Don't add an escape around the closing }. The other change is the substitution of \w with [A-Za-z0-9_].

▨**See Also** 2-11, 2-12, 2-13, 4-7, 4-12, 4-21, 6-18

4-12. Validating URLs

This recipe will validate a uniform resource locator (URL) as entered by a user. It will work on URLs that begin with http, https, ftp, or ftps. It stops at the hostname and doesn't work with full URL paths such as http://my.example.com/file.html.

Perl

```perl
#!/usr/bin/perl -w
use strict;

my $input = $ARGV[0];

if ( $input =~ /^(?:(?:http|ftp)s?):\/\/(?:[a-z0-9][-a-z0-9]+\.)+[a-z]{2,4}$/i )
{
    print "URL '" . $input . "' is valid\n";
} else {
    print "Please enter a valid URL!\n";
}
```

How It Works

In this expression, you may recognize the expression for checking hostnames from other recipes in this book. I cover the expression (?:[a-z0-9][-a-z0-9]+\.)+[a-z]{2,4} in quite a bit more detail in recipe 4-11. This expression has another expression tacked onto the beginning of it to catch http or ftp. The expression breaks down as follows:

(?:	a noncapturing group containing . . .
(?:	another noncapturing group that has . . .
http	*h*, *t*, *t*, and *p* . . .
|	or . . .
ftp	*f*, *t*, and *p* . . .
)	the end of the noncapturing group . . .
s	an *s* . . .
?	appearing at most once . . .
)	the end of the outermost noncapturing group.

PHP

```
<html>
<head><title>4-12 Validating URLs</title></head>
<style>
    .err { color : red ; font-weight : bold }
</style>
<body>
<form action="recipe4-12.php" method="post">
<input type="text" name="input" /><br/>
<input type="submit" value="Submit Form" /><br/><br/>
<?php
if ( $_SERVER['REQUEST_METHOD'] == "POST" )
{
    $input = $_POST['input'];
    if ( preg_match( "/^(?:(?:http|ftp)s?):\/\/(?:[a-z0-9][-a-z0-9]+\.)
+[a-z]{2,4}$/i", $input ) )
    {
        # Do some processing here - input if valid
    }
    else
    {
        print "<span class=\"err\">Bad URL.  Please correct and " .
            "resubmit the form</span><br/>";
    }
}
?>
</form>
</body>
</html>
```

How It Works

I describe this expression in further detail under "How It Works" in the Perl example of this recipe. It has the same limitation as the Perl example with full URLs that include path names.

Shell Scripting

```
$ grep -i -E '^((http|ftp)s?)://([a-z0-9][-a-z0-9]+\.)+[a-z]{2,4}$' filename
```

How It Works

POSIX-extended expressions don't support noncapturing groups in the form of (?:, so here I've used regular parentheses to group expressions. Like the other expressions, it matches URLs that don't have path names.

Vim

```
/^\(\(http\|ftp\)s\?\):\/\/\([a-z0-9][-a-z0-9]\+\.\)\+[a-z]\{2,4}$
```

How It Works

To walk through this expression, see "How It Works" under the Perl example of this recipe. Just remember that in Vim expressions, the (,), {, ?, and + characters are escaped to make them metacharacters. Also, I've replaced nongrouping parentheses with regular parentheses in this expression. Check the description of this recipe for limitations.

See Also 1-9, 2-1, 2-11, 2-12, 2-13, 2-14, 2-15, 4-3, 4-10, 4-11, 4-17, 6-12, 6-18, 6-19

4-13. Validating U.S. Phone Numbers

You can use this recipe to validate a U.S. phone number, with flexibility. It allows a phone number to have no formatting, to start with a 1 for long distance, and to have spaces or hyphens separating the parts. These are valid numbers: 1-800-555-4444, 555-333-4444, 5556663333, (555) 333-4444, and 555.333.4444. These aren't valid numbers: 555-4444, 1-800-555-OINK, 800#555#3333, and 555-555.

Perl

```perl
#!/usr/bin/perl -w
use strict;

my $input = $ARGV[0] || die "I have a bad feeling about this";

if ( $input =~  /^(?:1[- .]?)?\(?(?\d{3}\)?[- .]?\d{3}[- .]?\d{4}$/ )
{
    print "Phone number '" . $input . "' is valid\n";
} else {
    print "Please enter a valid phone number!\n";
}
```

How It Works

This recipe looks for groups or numbers or digits, identified here by the \d character class, with certain optional delimiters such as spaces, dots, or dashes. It also allows the parentheses that sometimes occur around the area code to be optional. The expression breaks down as follows:

^	the beginning of the line . . .
(?:	a noncapturing group . . .
1	a one . . .
[- .]	a character class that matches a dash, a space, or a dot . . .
?	that can appear at most once . . .
)	the end of the noncapturing group . . .
?	where this group can appear at most once . . .
\(	a literal parenthesis . . .
?	found optionally one time . . .
\d	a digit . . .
{3}	occurring three times . . .
\)	a literal parenthesis . . .

?	found at most once . . .
[- .]	a character class . . .
?	at most once . . .
\d	a digit . . .
{3}	found three times . . .
[- .]	the same character class seen earlier . . .
?	found zero or one time . . .
\d	a digit . . .
{4}	found four times . . .
$	the end of the line.

PHP

```php
<html>
<head><title>4-13 Validating US phone numbers</title></head>
<style>
    .err { color : red ; font-weight : bold }
</style>
<body>
<form action="recipe4-13.php" method="post">
<input type="text" name="input" /><br/>
<input type="submit" value="Submit Form" /><br/><br/>
<?php
if ( $_SERVER['REQUEST_METHOD'] == "POST" )
{
    $input = $_POST['input'];
    if ( preg_match( "/^(?:1[- .]?)?\(?(?\d{3}\)?[- .]?\d{3}[- .]?\d{4}$/",
        $input ) )
    {
        # Do some processing here - input if valid
    }
    else
    {
        print "<span class=\"err\">Bad phone number.  Please correct " .
            "and resubmit the form</span><br/>";
    }
}
?>
</form>
</body>
</html>
```

How It Works

Refer to the "How It Works" section under the Perl example to see how this expression breaks down.

Shell Scripting

```
$ grep -E '^(1[- .]?)?\(?[0-9]{3}\)?[- .]?[0-9]{3}[- .]?[0-9]{4}$' filename
```

How It Works

The \d character class that's used to match numbers in PCREs is replaced with [0-9] in this POSIX-extended expression. To see what makes this expression tick, refer to "How It Works" under the Perl example in this recipe.

Vim

```
/^\(1[- .]\?\)\?(\?\d\{3}\)\?[- .]\?\d\{3}[- .]\?\d\{4}$
```

How It Works

This expression is based on the PCREs, with the exception of escapes before (,), ?, and {. See the Perl example for an in-depth explanation of the expression.

■ **See Also** 1-4, 2-2, 2-3, 2-11, 2-13, 4-1, 4-2, 4-10, 4-18, 4-22, 4-23, 5-1, 5-2, 5-4, 6-3, 6-8, 6-13, 6-15

4-14. Validating U.S. Social Security Numbers

This recipe validates U.S. Social Security numbers. The number format itself is fairly straight-forward—it consists of a three-digit area code, followed by a two-digit group code, and finally followed by a four-digit serial number. This recipe takes it a step further and makes sure the area number is somewhat accurate. According to http://www.ssa.gov/employer/highgroup.txt, the highest current group number is 772, 000 is invalid, and several ranges exist between 000–772 in which numbers are currently unassigned. As of the time of this writing, the valid numbers for the area number are 001–665, 667–690, 700–733, 750, and 764–772.

Perl

```perl
#!/usr/bin/perl -w
use strict;

my $input = $ARGV[0] || die "Please supply a valid social security number.";

if ( $input =~  /^(00[1-9]|0[1-9]\d|[1-5]\d{2}|6[0-5]\d|66[0-5]| ⤸
66[7-9]|6[7-8]\d|690|7[0-2]\d|73[0-3]|750|76[4-9]|77[0-2])- ⤸
(?!00)\d{2}-(?!0000)\d{4}$/ )
{
    print "The number you entered is valid!\n";
}
else
{
    print "Please enter a valid number!\n";
}
```

How It Works

This recipe is the longest and most difficult to read example in this book that deals with ranges. Since they're explained in greater detail elsewhere, I'll point out what makes this recipe different from most of the others—the (?! operator you see in the second and third groups previously.

　　The operator excludes the groups 00 and 0000 from the second and third groups of numbers, respectively. The expression breaks down as follows:

(?!　　a group that doesn't contain . . .

00　　zero followed by zero . . .

)　　the end of the group . . .

\d　　a digit . . .

{2}　　found exactly two times.

PHP

```
<html>
<head><title>4-14 Validating US Social Security Numbers</title></head>
<style>
    .err { color : red ; font-weight : bold }
</style>
<body>
<form action="recipe4-14.php" method="post">
<input type="text" name="input"
    value="<? print $_POST['input']; ?>" /><br/>
<input type="submit" value="Submit Form" /><br/><br/>
<?php
if ( $_SERVER['REQUEST_METHOD'] == "POST" )
{
    $input = $_POST['input'];
    if ( preg_match( "/^(00[1-9]|0[1-9]\d|[1-5]\d{2}|6[0-5]\d|66[0-5]| ⤸
66[7-9]|6[7-8]\d|690|7[0-2]\d|73[0-3]|750|76[4-9]|77[0-2])- ⤸
(?!00)\d{2}-(?!0000)\d{4}$/", $input ) )
    {
        # Do some processing here - input if valid
        print "Looks good to me!<br/>";
    }
    else
    {
        print "<span class=\"err\">Invalid social security number!</span><br/>";
    }
}
?>
</form>
</body>
</html>
```

How It Works

For information about how this expression validates U.S. Social Security numbers, see "How It Works" under the Perl example in this recipe.

Shell Scripting

```
$ grep '^\(00[1-9]\|0[1-9][0-9]\|[1-5][0-9][0-9]\|6[0-5][0-9]\|66[0-5]\| ⤸
66[7-9]\|6[7-8][0-9]\|690\|7[0-2][0-9]\|73[0-3]\|750\|76[4-9]\|77[0-2]\)- ⤸
\([0[1-9]\|[1-9][0-9]\)-\(000[1-9]\|00[1-9][0-9]\|0[1-9][0-9]\{2\}\| ⤸
[1-9][0-9]\{3\}\)$' filename
```

How It Works

The previous grep example turns hideous only because the convenient (?! operator found in PCRE isn't available, so the exclusion of 00 and 0000 in the second and third groups must be done with ranges. Doing the ranges makes the expression longer and more difficult to read, but it still works the same.

Vim

```
/^\(00[1-9]\|0[1-9][0-9]\|[1-5][0-9][0-9]\|6[0-5][0-9]\|66[0-5]\|66[7-9]\| ↵
6[7-8][0-9]\|690\|7[0-2][0-9]\|73[0-3]\|750\|76[4-9]\|77[0-2]\)-\([0[1-9]\| ↵
[1-9][0-9]\)-\(000[1-9]\|00[1-9][0-9]\|0[1-9][0-9]\{2}\|[1-9][0-9]\{3}\)$
```

How It Works

The same expression used in the grep example works wonderfully in Vim (and vi). To make the expression a little shorter in Vim, you can take advantage of Vim's support of the \d character class to denote [0-9].

See Also 2-1, 2-15, 4-3, 4-10, 4-16, 4-17, 6-12, 6-19

FORMATTING AND VALIDATING

4-15. Validating Credit Card Numbers

You can use this recipe to validate credit card numbers entered by a user. It validates the number in groups, such as 4444-4444-4444-4444, with or without the dashes or with spaces instead.

Perl

```
#!/usr/bin/perl -w
use strict;

my $ccnumber = $ARGV[0] || die "No parameter given.";

if ( $ccnumber =~ /^(?:\d{4}[- ]?){3}\d{4}$/ )
{
    print "Looks good to me...\n";
} else {
    print "You can't buy anything with that...\n";
}
```

How It Works

This expression works by breaking the credit card number into four groups of numbers—each either followed by -, a space, nothing, or the end of the line. The group breaks down as follows:

^	the start of the line ...
(?:	a noncapturing group that contains ...
\d	a digit ...
{4}	found four times ...
[-]	a character class containing a hyphen and a space ...
?	that's optional ...
)	the end of the noncapturing group ...
{3}	found three times ...
\d	a digit ...
{4}	found four times ...
$	the end of the line.

PHP

```
<html>
<head><title>4-15 Validating credit cards</title></head>
<style>
    .err { color : red ; font-weight : bold }
</style>
<body>
<form action="recipe4-15.php" method="post">
<input type="text" name="input" /><br/>
<input type="submit" value="Submit Form" /><br/><br/>
<?php
if ( $_SERVER['REQUEST_METHOD'] == "POST" )
{
    $input = $_POST['input'];
    if ( preg_match( "/^(?:\d{4}[- ]?){3}\d{4}$/", $input ) )
    {
        # Do some processing here - input if valid
    }
    else
    {
        print "<span class=\"err\">This number doesn't look right</span><br/>";
    }
}
?>
</form>
</body>
</html>
```

How It Works

I describe this expression in detail under "How It Works" in the Perl example of this recipe.

Shell Scripting

```
$ grep -E '^([0-9]{4}[- ]?){3}[0-9]{4}$' filename
```

How It Works

The expression breaks down like this:

^	the beginning of the line . . .
(	a group that contains . . .
[0-9]	any number zero through nine . . .
{4}	four times . . .

[-]	a dash or a space . . .
?	appearing at most once . . .
)	the end of the group . . .
{3}	all appearing three times . . .
[0-9]	any number zero through nine . . .
{4}	four times . . .
$	the end of the line.

Vim

`/^\(\d\{4}[- ]\?\)\{3}\d\{4}$`

How It Works

This expression, which can be used to search through a file using Vim, breaks down into the following:

^	the beginning of the line . . .
\(	a group that contains . . .
\d	any number zero through nine . . .
\{4}	four times . . .
[-]	a dash or space . . .
\?	appearing at most once . . .
\)	the end of the group . . .
\{3}	all appearing three times . . .
[-]	a dash or a space . . .
\d	any number zero through nine . . .
{4}	four times . . .
$	the end of the line.

4-16. Validating Dates in MM/DD/YYYY

This expression validates dates in MM/DD/YYYY format. It goes a little further than just looking for digits—it will validate 1–12 for the MM, 1–31 for the date, and any four-digit number for the year.

Perl

```perl
#!/usr/bin/perl -w
use strict;

my $date = $ARGV[0];

if ( $date =~ /^(?:0?[1-9]|1[0-2])\/(?:0?[1-9]|[1-2]\d|3[0-1])\/(?:\d{4})$/ )
{
        print "Looks good to me...\n";
} else {
        print "Please enter a VALID date!\n";
}
```

How It Works

The bulk of this expression is breaking down the month and date into ranges so they can be validated. Each part of the expression (the three parts that validate the MM, DD, and YYYY parts of the year) is separated by \/, which matches a literal slash /.

The following is the first part of the expression, (?:0?[1-9]|1[0-2]), broken down:

(?:	a noncapturing group . . .
0	a zero . . .
?	at most one time . . .
[1-9]	one through nine . . .
|	or . . .
1	a one . . .
[0-2]	one through two . . .
)	the end of the noncapturing group.

It captures 1–12, with an optional zero in front of the single-digit numbers so dates such as 03/13/2004 are OK.

The second group validates numbers 1–31 and allows a zero in front of numbers less than 10. It breaks down like so:

(?:	a noncapturing group containing . . .
0	an optional zero, in front of . . .
[1-9]	one through nine . . .
|	or . . .
[1-2]	one through two in front of . . .
[\d]	any digit . . .
|	or . . .
3	a three . . .
[0-1]	zero through one.

The last group, which matches the year, is a lot more straightforward. It simply matches any set of four digits.

PHP

```
<html>
<head><title>4-16 Validating dates in MM/DD/YYYY</title></head>
<style>
        .err { color : red ; font-weight : bold }
</style>
<body>
<form action="recipe4-16.php" method="post">
<input type="text" name="input" value="<? $_POST['input']; ?>" /><br/>
<input type="submit" value="Submit Form" /><br/><br/>
<?php
if ( $_SERVER['REQUEST_METHOD'] == "POST" )
{
        $input = $_POST['input'];
        if ( preg_match( "/^(?:0?[1-9]|1[0-2])\/(?:0?[1-9]|[1-2]\d|↵
3[0-1])\/(?:\d{4})$/", $input ) )
        {
                # Do some processing here - input if valid
        }
        else
        {
                print "<span class=\"err\">Indy!  Bad dates...  </span><br/>";
        }
}
?>
```

```
</form>
</body>
</html>
```

How It Works

To see how this expression works, refer to "How It Works" under the Perl example in this recipe.

Shell Scripting

```
$ grep -E '^(0?[1-9]|1[0-2])/(0?[1-9]|[1-2][0-9]|3[0-1])/[0-9]{4}$' filename
```

How It Works

This POSIX expression is different from the PCREs given in the Perl and PHP examples in two ways. One is the replacement of \d with [0-9]; the other is the removal of noncapturing parentheses.

Vim

```
/^\(0\?[1-9]\|1[0-2]\)\/\(0\?[1-9]\|[1-2][0-9]\|3[0-1]\)\/[0-9]\{4}$
```

How It Works

To see how this expression works, take a look at the explanation with the Perl example. This one differs only with the extra escape characters before (,), ?, |, and {.

See Also 2-1, 2-15, 4-3, 4-10, 4-14, 4-17, 6-12

FORMATTING AND VALIDATING

4-17. Validating Times

This recipe validates times on a 12-hour clock. The times 12:00 PM, 12:21 P.M., and 1:38 A.M. are valid; 13:00 PM and 12:67 A.M. aren't valid. Seconds are allowed (12:32:12 P.M. is valid). This expression is case sensitive, so 12:00 PM will match, but 12:00 p.m. won't. See "Variations" at the end of this recipe for tips on how to make the match case insensitive.

Perl

```perl
#!/usr/bin/perl -w
use strict;

my $time = $ARGV[0];

if ( $time =~ /^(?:0?[1-9]|1[0-2]):(?:[0-5][0-9])(?::[0-5][0-9])? [PA]\.?M\.?$/ )
{
    print "Looks good to me...\n";
} else {
    print "What time is it?\n";
}
```

How It Works

The bulk of this expression is for limiting the numbers—the hours need to be less than 12, and the minutes need to be less than 60. The expression for validating numbers less than 12 is (?:1[0-2]|0?\d), which means the following:

(?:	a noncapturing group that contains . . .
1	a one followed by . . .
[0-2]	anything between zero and two . . .
|	or . . .
0	a zero . . .
?	that's optional, followed by . . .
[1-9]	one through nine . . .
)	the end of the noncapturing group.

The group that catches 00–59, the minutes part of the time, is (?:[0-5][0-9]). You'll see it twice in this expression, once again for the optional seconds part of the time.

You can find the full walk-through of the expression under "How It Works" in the PHP example of this recipe.

PHP

```
<html>
<head><title>4-17 Validating times</title></head>
<style>
    .err { color : red ; font-weight : bold }
</style>
<body>
<form action="recipe4-17.php" method="post">
<input type="text" name="input" /><br/>
<input type="submit" value="Submit Form" /><br/><br/>
<?php
if ( $_SERVER['REQUEST_METHOD'] == "POST" )
{
    $input = $_POST['input'];
    if ( preg_match( "/^(?:0?[1-9]|1[0-2]):(?:[0-5][0-9])↵
(?::[0-5][0-9])? [PA]\.?M\.?$/", $input ) )
    {
        # Do some processing here - input if valid
    }
    else
    {
        print "<span class=\"err\">Invalid time.</span><br/>";
    }
}
?>
</form>
</body>
</html>
```

How It Works

The crux of this expression, and also what makes it so verbose, is the splitting up of numbers to make sure the time given is within the appropriate ranges. To make this expression easier to digest, I'll break it down into four parts: the hour portion, the minutes expression, the optional seconds expression, and the p.m./a.m. expression. The following is a breakdown of the hour portion of the expression:

(?:	a noncapturing group containing . . .
0	a zero . . .
?	that's optional, followed by . . .
[1-9]	any number one through nine . . .
		or . . .
1	a one followed by . . .
[0-2]	anything from zero to two.

FORMATTING AND VALIDATING

That will catch anything 1–12. The next group, as follows, will match numbers 00–59:

(?:   a noncapturing group containing . . .

[0-5]   any number zero through five, followed by . . .

[0-9]   any number zero through nine . . .

)   the end of the noncapturing group.

This group is repeated with a ? at the end of it for the seconds expression to make it optional, and a colon is added in the group to properly separate minutes from seconds. The last group, which matches either A.M. or P.M., is as follows:

(?:   a noncapturing group containing . . .

[PA]   a *P* or *A*, then . . .

\.   a literal period (.) . . .

?   which may or may not be found . . .

M   an *M*, followed by . . .

\.   a literal period . . .

?   that's optional . . .

)   the end of the noncapturing group.

This expression allows PM, P.M., AM, and A.M. The /i option in the expression tells PHP to ignore the case in the string, so lowercase versions of the abbreviations will also match.

Shell Scripting

```
grep -E '^(0?[1-9]|1[0-2]):([0-5][0-9])(:[0-5][0-9])? [PA]\.?M\.?$' filename
```

How It Works

This expression is the same as the PCREs given in the Perl and PHP examples with the exception of (?:, noncapturing groups, being replaced by (. Other than that, you can follow through the expression under the "How It Works" section in the Perl example.

Vim

```
/^\(0\?[1-9]\|1[0-2]\):\([0-5][0-9]\)\(:[0-5][0-9]\)\? [PA]\.\?M\.\?$
```

How It Works

To see how this expression breaks down, see "How It Works" under the Perl example. The only difference between this expression and the Perl expression are the added escapes before (,), ?, and |.

Variations

You may be in a situation where you need to validate a 24-hour time instead of a 12-hour time like the one shown in this recipe. If that's the case, you can easily modify this recipe to validate for 24-hour times. You won't need the a.m. or p.m. checks anymore, and you'll need to modify the ranges to allow for any number 00–24, like so:

```
^(?:0[1-9]|1[0-9]|2[0-3]):(?:[0-5][0-9])(?::[0-5][0-9])?
```

You may also want to ignore case in the a.m. or p.m. matches so a.m. or p.m. is valid. To allow Perl to become case insensitive, use the i qualifier at the end of the match. For grep, use the -i parameter.

To ignore case in Vim, use \c anywhere in the expression. I always tack it on at the end to make sure to keep it separate from the main part of the expression.

See Also 2-1, 2-15, 4-3, 4-10, 4-14, 4-17, 6-12

4-18. Validating U.S. Postal Codes

You can use this recipe to validate U.S. postal codes. It accepts ZIP+4 codes as an option. The numbers 55555-5555 and 55555 are valid, but 444 and 444-4444 aren't.

Perl

```perl
#!/usr/bin/perl -w
use strict;

my $date = $ARGV[0];

if ( $date =~ /^\d{5}(?:-\d{4})?$/ )
{
    print "Looks good to me...\n";
} else {
    print "I need a VALID postal code!\n";
}
```

How It Works

This expression looks for five digits, which make up U.S. postal codes. It also allows the +4 portion of the postal code to be added with a dash separating the two. The details are as follows:

^	the beginning of the line . . .
\d	a number . . .
{5}	found five times, followed by . . .
(?:	a noncapturing group containing . . .
-	a dash . . .
\d	a number . . .
{4}	found four times . . .
)	the end of the noncapturing group . . .
?	which is optional, then . . .
$	the end of the line.

PHP

```html
<html>
<head><title>4-18 Validating US postal codes</title></head>
<style>
```

```
    .err { color : red ; font-weight : bold }
</style>
<body>
<form action="recipe4-18.php" method="post">
<input type="text" name="input" /><br/>
<input type="submit" value="Submit Form" /><br/><br/>
<?php
if ( $_SERVER['REQUEST_METHOD'] == "POST" )
{
    $input = $_POST['input'];
    if ( preg_match( "/^\d{5}(?:-\d{4})?$/", $input ) )
    {
        # Do some processing here - input if valid
    }
    else
    {
        print "<span class=\"err\">Try again.</span><br/>";
    }
}
?>
</form>
</body>
</html>
```

How It Works

I cover this expression under "How It Works" in the Perl example of this recipe.

Shell Scripting

```
$ grep -E '^[0-9]{5}(-[0-9]{4})?$' file
```

How It Works

The \d character class is replaced by [0-9] in this POSIX expression to make it slightly different from the PCREs in the Perl and PHP examples. For more details about how this expression works, see the Perl example in this recipe.

Vim

```
/^[0-9]\{5}\(-[0-9]\{4}\)\?$
```

How It Works

This expression is similar to the PCRE expressions in this recipe, with the exception of the escaped {, (,), and ?. See "How It Works" under the Perl example for details on this expression.

FORMATTING AND VALIDATING

4-19. Extracting Usernames from E-mail Addresses

You can use this recipe to grab the username out of an e-mail address. Given myname@example.com, the result will be myname.

Perl

```
#!/usr/bin/perl -w
use strict;

my $username = $ARGV[0];

if ( $username =~ s/^([^@]+)(@.*)$/$1/ )
{
    print "$username\n";
} else {
    print "I couldn't determine your hostname...\n";
}
```

How It Works

This expression works to extract a username from an e-mail address because it grabs everything up to the @ in one group and holds everything including and after the @ to the end of the line in another group. In the expression, it simply drops the second group so everything after @ goes nowhere.

■**Note** This expression doesn't validate the address. For more about e-mail address validation, see recipe 4-11.

The following is the expression, broken down into parts:

^   the beginning of the line . . .

(a capturing group containing . . .

[^@]   everything that isn't an at (@) sign . . .

+   found one or more times, up to . . .

(another group containing . . .

@   an at sign (@) . . .

.   any character

*   found zero, one, or many times . . .

)   the end of the group . . .

$ the end of the line.

PHP

```
<html>
<head><title>4-19 Extracting usernames from e-mail addresses</title></head>
<style>
    .err { color : red ; font-weight : bold }
</style>
<body>
<form action="recipe4-19.php" method="post">
<input type="text" name="input" /><br/>
<input type="submit" value="Submit Form" /><br/><br/>
<?php
if ( $_SERVER['REQUEST_METHOD'] == "POST" )
{
    $input = $_POST['input'];
    if (preg_match ( "/^([^@]+)(@.*)$/", $input ) )
    {
        # Do some processing here - input if valid
        $username = preg_replace( "/^([^@]+)(@.*)$/", "$1", $input);
        print "<b>Found username \"$username\"</b>";
    }
    else
    {
        print "<span class=\"err\">No username found here:</span><br/>";
    }
}
?>
</form>
</body>
</html>
```

How It Works

I give the details of this expression in the "How It Works" section under the Perl example of this recipe.

Shell Scripting

```
$ sed 's/^\([^@]\+\)\(@.*\)$/\1/g' filename
```

How It Works

This sed command, used for making replacements, uses the back reference \1 to print what was captured in the first group and drop what was found in the second group. This expression is identical to the one covered in "How It Works" in the Perl example.

Vim

```
:%s/^\([^@]\+\)\(@.*\)$/\1/g
```

How It Works

To see the search expression broken down, refer to "How It Works" under the Perl example. Remember that (,), and + are escaped with \ to give them their special meaning, which is opposite from most regular expression flavors.

■**See Also** 1-7, 1-17, 2-2, 2-3, 2-6, 2-9, 3-1, 3-2, 3-3, 3-4, 4-6, 5-3, 5-4, 5-5, 5-6, 5-7, 6-1, 6-2, 6-22

FORMATTING AND VALIDATING

4-20. Extracting Dialing Codes from International Phone Numbers

You can use this expression to extract the dialing code from an international phone number. It assumes the dialing code starts after the plus (+) sign and goes up to the first space or hyphen for a maximum of three characters. Given +011 1-555-333-4444, it will extract 011.

Perl

```
#!/usr/bin/perl -w
use strict;

my $number = $ARGV[0];

if ( $number =~ s/^\+(\d{1,3})([- ]+.*)$/$1/ )
{
    print "Your dialing code is '". $number ."'\n";
} else {
    print "I didn't find a dialing code.\n";
}
```

How It Works

By capturing everything after the dialing code but not putting it back in the replacement, this expression drops all but what was found as the dialing code. The following is the search expression, broken down:

^	the beginning of the line . . .
\+	a literal plus (+) . . .
(	a group that captures . . .
\d	a digit . . .
{1,3}	one to three times, up to . . .
)	the end of the group . . .
(	a group that captures . . .
[-]	a hyphen or a space . . .
+	found zero or one time, followed by . . .
.	any character . . .
*	found zero or more times . . .
)	the end of the group . . .
$	until the end of the line.

PHP

```
<html>
<head><title>4-20 Extracting an international dialing code</title></head>
<style>
    .err { color : red ; font-weight : bold }
</style>
<body>
<form action="recipe4-20.php" method="post">
<input type="text" name="input" /><br/>
<input type="submit" value="Submit Form" /><br/><br/>
<?php
if ( $_SERVER['REQUEST_METHOD'] == "POST" )
{
    $input = $_POST['input'];
    if ( preg_match ( "/^\+(\d{1,3})([- ]?.*)$/", $input ) )
    {
        # Do some processing here - input if valid
        $dialingcode = preg_replace ( "/^\+(\d{1,3})([- ]?.*)$/",
            "$1", $input );
        print "<b>Found code '$dialingcode'</b>";
    }
    else
    {
        print "<span class=\"err\">I didn't find a dialing code<span><br/>";
    }
}
?>
</form>
</body>
</html>
```

How It Works

To see a detailed explanation about how this expression works, refer to "How It Works" under the Perl example of this recipe.

Shell Scripting

```
$ sed -r 's/^\+([0-9]{1,3})([- ]+.*)$/\1/g' file
```

How It Works

To see a detailed explanation about how this expression works, refer to "How It Works" under the Perl example of this recipe.

Vim

```
:%s/^+\([0-9]\{1,3}\)\([- ]\+.*\)$/\1/g
```

How It Works

To see a detailed explanation about how this expression works, refer to "How It Works" under the Perl example of this recipe.

4-21. Reformatting People's Names (First Name, Last Name)

This expression will look at a string and try to parse it as a proper name given in firstname lastname format. If it finds a suitable match, it will rewrite the name as lastname, firstname.

Perl

```
#!/usr/bin/perl -w
use strict;

my $name = $ARGV[0];

$name =~ s/^(.*)\s([a-z']+)$/$2, $1/i;
print "'" . $name ."'\n";
```

How It Works

This expression breaks down like this:

^	the beginning of the line . . .
(	a group that captures . . .
.	any character . . .
*	zero, one, or many times . . .
)	the end of the group . . .
\s	some whitespace . . .
(	another capturing group . . .
[A-z']	the letters *A* through *z* and ' . . .
+	one or more times . . .
)	the end of the second group . . .
$	the end of the line.

The i option is used here to make the [a-z'] range case insensitive. See the "Syntax Overview" section earlier in the book for more details.

PHP

```
<html>
<head><title>4-21 Reformatting peoples' names
    (first name, last name)</title></head>
<style>
    .err { color : red ; font-weight : bold }
</style>
<body>
<form action="recipe4-21.php" method="post">
<input type="text" name="input" /><br/>
<input type="submit" value="Submit Form" /><br/><br/>
<?php
if ( $_SERVER['REQUEST_METHOD'] == "POST" )
{
    $input = $_POST['input'];
    if ( $name = preg_replace( "/^(.*)\s([A-Za-z']+)$/",
        "$2, $1", $input ) )
    {
        # Do some processing here - input if valid
        print "<b>Filing under: '$name'</b>";
    }
    else
    {
        print "<span class=\"err\">I didn't change anything<span><br/>";
    }
}
?>
</form>
</body>
</html>
```

How It Works

To read more about the details of this expression, see "How It Works" under the Perl example of this recipe.

Shell Scripting

```
$ sed -r 's/^(.*)[[:space:]]([A-Za-z]+)$/\2, \1/g' filename
```

How It Works

For details about this expression, see "How It Works" under the Perl example. Remember that \s isn't supported in POSIX-extended expressions, so here [[:space:]] is used instead.

Vim

```
%s/^\(.*\)\s\([A-Za-z']\+\)$/\2, \1/
```

How It Works

With the exception of the escaped (,), +, and ? in this expression, the expression is identical to the Perl and PHP expressions. For details about what makes this expression function, see "How It Works" under the Perl example.

See Also 2-11, 2-12, 2-13, 2-14, 4-7, 4-11, 4-12, 6-18

4-22. Finding Addresses with Post Office Boxes

Some input may require a street address, especially when shipping information is required. This recipe catches PO, P.O., and Box to catch addresses, so an application can warn users if there appears to be a post office box address instead of a street address.

Perl

```perl
#!/usr/bin/perl -w
use strict;

my $input = $ARGV[0];

if ( $input =~ /^(?:P\.?O\.?\s)?(?:BOX)\b/i )
{
        print "The address provided looks like a post office box\n";
} else {
        print "Shipping to '" . $input . "'\n";
}
```

How It Works

This expression operates on the assumption that an address that starts with Box, PO Box, or P.O. Box isn't a street address. If the match succeeds, the previous script spits out a message to the screen. Otherwise, it tells you it's happily shipping to the address you've provided.

The expression breaks down like this:

^	the beginning of the line . . .
(?:	a noncapturing group containing . . .
P	a *P* . . .
\.	a period . . .
?	that's optional . . .
O	an *O* . . .
\.	a period . . .
?	that's optional . . .
)	the end of the noncapturing group . . .
?	where the previous group is optional . . .
(?:	a noncapturing group that contains . . .
BOX	*B*, *O*, and then *X* . . .
)	the end of the noncapturing group . . .
\b	a word boundary.

PHP

```
<html>
<head><title>4-22 Finding addresses with post office boxes</title></head>
<style>
    .err { color : red ; font-weight : bold }
</style>
<body>
<form action="recipe4-22.php" method="post">
<input type="text" name="input" /><br/>
<input type="submit" value="Submit Form" /><br/><br/>
<?php
if ( $_SERVER['REQUEST_METHOD'] == "POST" )
{
    $input = $_POST['input'];
    if ( preg_match( "/^(?:P\.?O\.?\s)?(?:BOX)/i", $input ) )
    {
        print "<span class=\"err\">Looks like a post office box!</span><br/>";
    }
    else
    {
        # Do some processing here - input if valid
    }
}
?>
</form>
</body>
</html>
```

How It Works

The preg_match() function in PHP provides a switch that allows the regular expression to be case insensitive, allowing the expression to be much more concise.

For a detailed look at the expression in this example, see "How It Works" under the Perl example in this recipe.

Shell Scripting

```
$ grep -E -i '^(P\.?O\.?[[:space:]])?(BOX)' filename
```

How It Works

Aside from [[:space:]] instead of \s as a character class that matches whitespace, you can read more about how this expression works in "How It Works" under the Perl example in this recipe.

The grep command uses the -i parameter to specify case insensitivity in the search.

Vim

```
/\c^\(P\.\?O\.\?\s\)\?BOX
```

How It Works

You can use the \c character class in a search to specify that the expression is case insensitive. I put it at the beginning of the expression to keep it separate from the rest of the search expression. Follow the walk-through in the "How It Works" section under the Perl example for more information about this expression.

4-23. Validating Affirmative Responses

You can use this recipe as a user-friendly method of detecting positive configuration values.
With this recipe, code for checking for True, true, Y, or Yes is unnecessary.

Perl

```perl
#!/usr/bin/perl -w
use strict;

my $str = $ARGV[0];

if ( $str =~ /^(?:t(?:rue)?|y(?:es)?)$/i )
{
    print "Yes!!\n";
}
else
{
    print "Uh, no.\n";
}

exit 0;
```

How It Works

This expression checks for true, t, yes, and y with case insensitivity. It can be handy when
checking for positive values without putting in a bunch of if...else statements in your code.
The following is the expression, broken down into parts:

^	the beginning of the line ...
(?:	a noncapturing group that contains ...
t	a *t* ...
(?:	a noncapturing group that has ...
rue	*r, u, e* ...
)	the end of the noncapturing group ...
?	found zero or one time ...
|	or ...
y	a *y* ...
(?:	a noncapturing group contains ...

e	an *e* ...
s	an *s* ...
)	the end of the noncapturing group ...
?	found zero or one time ...
)	the end of the outermost noncapturing group ...
$	the end of the line.

The i option makes the search case insensitive, so the expression doesn't have to include the uppercase and lowercase letters.

PHP

```
<html>
<head><title>4-23 Validating affirmative responses</title></head>
<style>
    .err { color : red ; font-weight : bold }
</style>
<body>
<form action="recipe4-23.php" method="post">
<input type="text" name="input" value="<? $_POST['input'];?>"/><br/>
<input type="submit" value="Submit Form" /><br/><br/>
<?php
if ( $_SERVER['REQUEST_METHOD'] == "POST" )
{
    $input = $_POST['input'];
    if ( preg_match( "/^(?:t(?:rue)?|y(?:es)?)$/i", $input ) )
    {
        print "<b>Yes!!</b>";
    }
    else
    {
        print "<b>Nope</b>";
    }
}
?>
</form>
</body>
</html>
```

How It Works
See "How It Works" under the Perl example in this recipe.

Shell Scripting

```
$ grep -i '^\(t\(rue\)\?\|y\(es\)\?\)$' filename
```

How It Works

See "How It Works" under the Perl example, but forget about the noncapturing groups. Remember to escape (,), |, and ?.

Vim

```
/^\%(t\%(rue\)\?\|y\%(es\)\?\)$\c
```

How It Works

The \c sequence in the Vim recipe makes it case insensitive. It can appear anywhere in the string, but I usually put it either at the end or at the beginning to make it easier to read. Other than that change, you can follow the recipe as explained in "How It Works" under the Perl example in this recipe.

■**See Also** 1-3, 1-4

CHAPTER 5

■ ■ ■

HTML and XML

This chapter contains recipes that work with Hypertext Markup Language (HTML) and Extensible Markup Language (XML) files. As you walk through this chapter, you'll see some similarities among the recipes, because many of them deal with HTML and XML tags.

Working with tags can be especially challenging for the regular expression beginner, because the < and > characters that open and close tags are similar to \< and \>, which are word boundaries in some Portable Operating System Interface (POSIX) implementations such as GNU grep and sed, as well as the Vim implementation.

Throughout this chapter, some of the recipes may not have examples in GNU grep, sed, or Vim; these take advantage of advanced features that only Perl-Compatible Regular Expressions (PCREs) support.

5-1. Removing Whitespace from HTML

This recipe removes whitespace between HTML tags. The following string:

```
<p>  <b>Bold words</b>    </p>
```

becomes

```
<p><b>Bold words</b></p>
```

One of reasons for eliminating whitespace in HTML pages is that whitespace between tags is just for readability. If you have a site that has a lot of hits, it's a good idea to consider cleaning up things such as extra whitespace in HTML. I've worked with Webmasters that have saved more than 500 megabytes (MB) being transferred a month just by cleaning whitespace and newline characters out of their HTML—and that's on a relatively small site!

Perl

```perl
#!/usr/bin/perl -w
use strict;

my $html = $ARGV[0];

$html =~ s/(?:(?<=\>)|(?<=\/\>))(\s+)(?=\<\/?)//g;
print "'" . $html . "'\n";
```

How It Works

The (\s+) group captures whitespace, which is replaced by nothing. The look-behinds (?<=\>) and (?<=\/\>) and the look-ahead (?=\<\/?) make sure the whitespace is between two tags but not inside them. Here are the details:

(?:	a noncapturing group that contains . . .
(?<=	a positive look-behind with . . .
\>	a > . . .
)	the end of the positive look-behind . . .
|	or . . .
(?<=	a positive look-behind with . . .
\/	a slash, followed by . . .
\>	a > . . .
)	the end of the positive look-behind . . .
)	the end of the noncapturing group . . .
(	a capturing group that contains . . .

\s	whitespace . . .
+	one time or more . . .
)	the end of the capturing group . . .
(?=	a positive look-ahead . . .
\<	a <, followed by . . .
\/	a slash . . .
?	that can occur at most once . . .
)	the end of the positive look-ahead.

PHP

```
<html>
<head><title>5-1 Removing whitespace from HTML</title></head>
<body>
<form action="recipe5-1.php" method="post">
<input type="text" name="html"
    value="<?php print $_POST['html'];?>" /><br />
<input type="submit" value="Remove whitespace" /><br /><br />
<?php
if ( $_SERVER['REQUEST_METHOD'] == "POST" )
{
    $html = $_POST['html'];
    $newhtml = preg_replace( "/(?:(?<=\>)|(?<=\/\>))(\s+)(?=\<\/?)/",
        "", $html );
    print "<b>Original text was:  '" . htmlspecialchars($html) .
        "'</b><br/>";
    print "<b>New text is:  '" . htmlspecialchars($newhtml) . "'</b><br/>";
}
?>
</form>
</body>
</html>
```

How It Works

To see how this expression breaks down, refer to the "How It Works" section under the Perl example.

The look-behind group (?:(?<=\>)|(?<=\/\>)) matches the end of an HTML tag. The reason (?<=\>|\/\>) doesn't work in the expression is because neither Perl nor PHP permits variable-length look-behinds. Each look-behind needs to be broken up by itself and put inside a group, such as (?:(?<=\>)|(?<\/\>)).

HTML AND XML

Shell Scripting

```
$ sed 's/\(\/\?>\)[[:space:]]\+\(<\/\?\)/\1\2/g' filename
```

How It Works

Since sed doesn't support using look-arounds, the back references \1 and \2 are used to put what's found in the groups back into the replacement string. The expression breaks down into the following:

\(	a group that contains . . .
\/	a slash . . .
\?	found one or more times . . .
>	a > . . .
\)	a closing group . . .
[[:space:]]	the whitespace character class . . .
\+	found one or more times . . .
\(	another group that contains . . .
<	a < . . .
\/	a slash . . .
\?	found at most one time . . .
\)	the end of the group.

The opening and closing tag parts captured in the two groups, \(\/\?>\) and \(<\/\?\), respectively, are put back into the replacement expression with \1 and \2.

Vim

`:%s/\(\/\?>\)\@<=\s\+\(<\/\?\)\@=//g`

How It Works

This expression, supported in Vim, breaks down as follows:

`\(`	the start of the look-behind group . . .
`\/`	a / . . .
`\?`	found at most one time . . .
`>`	a > . . .
`\)\@<=`	identifies the preceding group as a positive look-behind . . .
`\s`	whitespace . . .
`\+`	occurring one or more times . . .
`\(`	the start of another group that contains . . .
`<`	a < . . .
`\/`	a / . . .
`\?`	at most one time . . .
`\)`	the end of a group . . .
`\@=`	identifies the preceding group as a positive look-ahead.

The look-aheads in Vim, although in syntax a little quirky compared to those used in Perl, work by making sure the preceding or following expression is found, but they don't actually match anything. The advantage this provides is that back references don't have to be used to put captured text back in the replacement expression.

See Also 4-4, 4-6, 5-2, 5-3, 5-4

5-2. Removing Whitespace from CSS

This recipe removes whitespace from inside brackets in Cascading Style Sheet (CSS) files.
The following string:

```
p { font-family: verdana; font-size : 8pt }
```

becomes

```
p {font-family:serif;font-size:8pt}
```

This particular recipe requires look-arounds as it's written here. This recipe doesn't have a
shell scripting example, because POSIX implementations like those used in GNU grep don't
support look-arounds.

Perl

```
#!/usr/bin/perl -w
use strict;

my $html = $ARGV[0];

$html =~ s/(?<=[:;\w{])\s+(?=[}\w;:])//g;
print "'" . $html . "'\n";
```

How It Works

This expression uses a negative look-behind because look-behinds don't capture any text,
so the replacement expression doesn't have to use a back reference to put text back.

The look-behind expression is (?<=[:;\w{]). It will make the whitespace match as
long as it's preceded by :, ;, \w, or {. If you look at the example in the previous description,
p { font-family: verdana; font-size : 8pt }, you'll see that each one of the spaces
inside the brackets meets this criteria.

The look-ahead in the expression, (?=[}\w;:]), makes the whitespace group match only
if it's followed by }, \w, ;, or :. Every whitespace in the example also matches these criteria.

PHP

```
<html>
<head><title>5-2 Removing whitespace from CSS</title></head>
<body>
<form action="recipe5-2.php" method="post">
<input type="text" name="css"
    value="<?php print $_POST['css'];?>" /><br />
<input type="submit" value="Remove whitespace" /><br /><br />
<?php
if ( $_SERVER['REQUEST_METHOD'] == "POST" )
{
```

```
    $css = $_POST['css'];
    $newcss = preg_replace( "/(?<=[:;\w{])\s+(?=[}\w;:])/", "", $css );
    print "<b>Original text was:  '$css'</b><br/>";
    print "<b>New text is:  '$newcss'</b><br/>";
}
?>
</form>
</body>
</html>
```

How It Works

The entire regular expression breaks down here; if you want to know more about why the expression is made this way, see "How It Works" under the Perl example.

(?<=	a positive look-behind that contains . . .
[	a character class that will match . . .
:	a colon . . .
;	semicolon . . .
\w	a word character . . .
{	or opening bracket (it doesn't have to be escaped when it's in a character class) . . .
]	the end of the character class . . .
)	the end of the positive look-behind . . .
\s	whitespace . . .
+	found one or more times . . .
(?=	a positive look-ahead that contains . . .
[	a character class that matches . . .
}	a closing bracket . . .
\w	a word character . . .
;	a semicolon, or . . .
:	a colon . . .
]	the end of the character class . . .
)	the end of the positive look-ahead.

Using this expression, the spaces inside brackets will be replaced by an empty string, thus deleting the spaces. This is handy for making CSS a little tighter but not necessarily more readable.

Vim

`:%s/[:;A-Za-z0-9{]\@<=\s\+[}A-Za-z0-9;:]\@=//g`

How It Works

Look-arounds in this expression make sure the whitespace is inside brackets, and they make the replacement an empty string. The Vim expression breaks down as follows:

[…]   a character class . . .

\@<=   makes the preceding expression a look-behind . . .

\s   whitespace . . .

\+   found one or more times . . .

[…]   another character class . . .

\@=   that's a positive look-ahead.

The character classes are `[:;A-Za-z0-9{]` and `[}A-Za-z0-9;:]`. The first class looks for an opening bracket, a colon, a semicolon, and characters that could be parts of the CSS entries. The second character class differs only in that it includes a closing bracket instead of an opening bracket.

■**See Also** 4-4, 4-6, 5-1, 5-3, 5-4

5-3. Making HTML Tags Lowercase

This recipe takes advantage of special support offered in some regular expression engines to change the case of a back reference. Using this feature, you can make HTML tags lowercase. Text such as <HTML></HTML> becomes <html></html>.

This regular expression uses some features that aren't supported by all the languages featured in this book. In this recipe, Perl and Vim are the only examples that support this special feature.

Note Be careful with content inside <PRE></PRE> tags—this recipe won't check for them. Sometimes it isn't appropriate to change the case of HTML tags.

Perl

```perl
#!/usr/bin/perl -w
use strict;

open ( FILE, $ARGV[0] ) || die "Cannot open file!";

while (<FILE>)
{
    my $line = $_;
    $line =~ s/(?:(?<=\<)|(?<=\<\/))([^\/ >]+)(?=\/?\>| )/\L$1/g;
    print $line;
}

close( FILE );
```

How It Works

To make the text captured by the back reference ($1 previously) lowercase, the special option \L is used in the replacement expression immediately before the back reference.

The expression really consists of three different, smaller expressions. The first one is the expression that's used as a look-behind to make sure the grouping later will match only inside an HTML tag: (?:(?<=\<)|(?<=\<\/)). HTML tags can begin with < or </ if the tag is a closing tag. You can't use something such as </? to make the / optional in a back reference because many regular expression engines don't support variable-length look-behinds, including Perl. This is why it breaks down as follows:

(?:   a noncapturing group, that contains . . .

(?<=   a positive look-behind that has . . .

\<   a < (the start of an HTML tag) . . .

)   the end of the positive look-behind . . .

`|`	or . . .
`(?<=`	a different positive look-behind that contains . . .
`\<\/`	</ (the other way a tag can start) . . .
`)`	the end of the positive look-behind . . .
`)`	the end of the noncapturing group.

A second expression, (`[^\/ >]+`), matches the tag itself.

`(`	a group that contains . . .
`[^`	a character class that *doesn't* contain . . .
`\/`	a slash . . .
`<space>`	a space . . .
`\>`	or a > . . .
`]`	the end of the character class . . .
`+`	one or more times . . .
`)`	the end of the group.

You could match the tag name in more ways, but this one targets anything that isn't the close of a tag or a space, where whatever is matched is followed by the look-ahead.

The look-ahead in this expression is (`?=\/?\>|`), which is intended to match the end of an HTML tag name. This name can end with a space (`<br />`), a > (`<b>`), or the combination `/>` (`<br/>`). The look-ahead makes that work.

`(?=`	a positive look-ahead that contains . . .
`\/`	a slash . . .
`?`	occurring at most once . . .
`>`	a > that may end the tag name . . .
`|`	or . . .
`<space>`	a space . . .
`)`	the end of the positive look-ahead.

See Also 1-14

5-4. Removing an HTML Attribute

This recipe allows you to remove an HTML attribute from inside an HTML tag. It will ignore text that isn't inside an HTML tag. In these examples, the style attribute is being removed. The string <p style="font-size:8pt"> becomes just <p>.

Perl

```
#!/usr/bin/perl -w
use strict;

my $html = $ARGV[0];

$html =~ s/(?:(?<=\<)|(?<=\<\/))([^\/>]+)(?:\sstyle=['\"][^'\"]+?['\"])↵
([^\/>]*)(?=\/?\>| )/$1$2/g;
print "'" . $html . "'\n";
```

How It Works

This expression removes the style attribute by capturing everything before and after it inside the tag and uses back references to put the tag back together, omitting the attribute.

The expression consists of four smaller expressions. I discuss the first one, (?:(?<=\<)|(?<=\<\/)), in detail in recipe 5-3. The second group, ([^\/>]+), matches everything from the beginning of the tag up to the attribute. This will be put into the replacement string with the back reference $1. The expression breaks down into the following:

(	a group that contains . . .
[^	a character class that *doesn't* match . . .
\/	a slash . . .
>	or a > . . .
]	the end of the character class . . .
+	found one or more times . . .
)	the end of the group.

This expression just makes sure that what's there isn't the end of a tag. The third expression is a noncapturing group that matches the attribute, broken down into the following:

(?:	a noncapturing group that contains . . .
\s	whitespace . . .
style	an *s*, *t*, *y*, *l*, and *e* to match the style attribute . . .
=	an equal sign . . .
['\"]	a character class that matches a single quote or a double quote . . .

[^'\"]   a character class that *isn't* a single or a double quote . . .

+?   found one or more times, with a lazy qualifier, up to . . .

['\"]   a character class that matches a single or a double quote . . .

)   the end of the group.

Now for the fourth expression: ([^\/>]*). This one matches everything from the attribute to the end tag. (The end of the tag is defined by the last group.) The expression is simply an optional character class that will match anything except / and >.

The last expression is a look-ahead that defines the end of the HTML tag. Recipe 5-3 explains it in detail.

PHP

```
<html>
<head><title>5-4 Removing an HTML attribute</title></head>
<body>
<form action="recipe5-4.php" method="post">
<input type="text" name="str"
    value="<?php print htmlspecialchars($_POST['str']);?>" /><br />
<input type="submit" value="Remove style attribute" /><br /><br />
<?php
if ( $_SERVER['REQUEST_METHOD'] == "POST" )
{
    $str = $_POST['str'];
    $newstr = preg_replace( "/(?:(?<=\<)|(?<=\<\/))([^\/>]+)↵
(?:\sstyle=['\"][^'\"]+['\"])↵
([^\/>]*)(?=\/?\>| )/", "$1$2", $str );
    print "<b>Original text was:  '" . htmlspecialchars($str) .
        "'</b><br/>";
    print "<b>New text is:  '" . htmlspecialchars($newstr) .
        "'</b><br/>";
}
?>
</form>
</body>
</html>
```

How It Works
See "How It Works" under the Perl example for details about this expression.

Shell Scripting

```
$ sed 's/\(<\/\?[^\/>]\+\)[[:space:]]style=[\'"][^\'"]*[\'"]⏎
\(.*\/\?>\| \)/\1\2/g' filename
```

How It Works

The sed command doesn't support look-arounds, so the grouping parentheses are moved around to capture everything before and after the attribute, including the opening and closing of the HTML tag.

The first group, \(<\/\?[^\/>]\+\), matches everything up to the space before the attribute.

\(	a group that contains ...
<	a <, which opens the tag ...
\/	a / ...
\?	that can occur at most once ...
[^	a character class that doesn't match ...
\/	a slash or ...
>	the closing of an HTML tag ...
]	the end of the character class ...
\+	one or more times ...
\)	the end of the group.

The [[:space:]]style=[\'"[^\'"]*[\'"] syntax matches the attribute and whatever value it has assigned to it. The other group, \(.*\/\?>\| \), matches everything after the attribute up to the end of the HTML tag so it can be replaced by the \2 back reference.

\(	a group that contains ...
.	any character ...
*	zero, one, or many times ...
\/	a slash ...
\?	at most one time ...
>	a >, the end of the HTML tag ...
|	or ...
<space>	a space ...
\)	the end of the group.

When \1 and \2 are put back together, the attribute is dropped.

Vim

`:%s/\%(<\/\?\)\@<=\([^\/\>]\+\)\sstyle=['"[^'"]*['"]\(.*\)\%(\/\?>\| \)\@=/\1\2/g`

How It Works

The Vim recipe shown here uses look-arounds to make sure the summary attribute is inside an HTML tag. The look-around to find the beginning of the tag is `\%(<\/\?\)\@<=`, which breaks down as follows:

`\%(`	the beginning of a noncapturing group ...
`<`	the start of the HTML tag ...
`\/`	a slash ...
`\?`	that can occur at most one time ...
`\)`	the end of the noncapturing group ...
`\@<=`	the preceding group is a positive look-behind.

The next group captures everything from the beginning of the tag to the whitespace before the `style` attribute.

`\(`	the start of a group that contains ...
`[^`	a character class that *doesn't* match ...
`\/`	a / ...
`\>`	a > ...
`]`	the end of the character class ...
`\+`	one time or more ...
`\)`	the end of the group.

The next part of the expression catches the `style` attribute (and preceding space) and the attribute's value.

`\s`	whitespace ...
`style`	the attribute ...
`=`	an equal sign ...
`['"]`	a character class that matches either a single or double quote ...
`[^'"]`	a character that *isn't* a single or double quote ...
`*`	found zero, one, or many times up to ...
`['"]`	a character class that matches either a single or double quote.

Now you have to capture everything after the style attribute and value up to the end of the HTML tag.

\(	a group that contains . . .
.	any character . . .
*	found zero, one, or many times . . .
\)	the end of the group.

Finally, the last look-ahead searches for the end of the HTML tag.

\%(	a noncapturing group that captures . . .
\/	a slash . . .
\?	found at most one time . . .
>	a > . . .
|	or . . .
<space>	a space . . .
\)	the end of the noncapturing group . . .
\@=	the preceding expression is a look-ahead.

Variations

With a couple easy modifications, you can use this expression to replace HTML attributes with different attributes; for instance, you can replace the style attribute with a class attribute.

You can leave the search expression the same, (?:(?<=\<)|(?<=\<\/))([^\/>]+) (?:\sstyle=['\"][^'\"]+?['\"])([^\/>]*)(?=\/?\>|), and change the replacement expression to something such as $1 class="myClass" $2.

5-5. Searching for HTML Attributes

This expression allows you to search for an HTML attribute. It ignores the text outside HTML tags. The examples here are looking for the summary attribute. The string

```
<table summary="My table">
```

will match, while the string

```
<p>summary=""</p>
```

won't match.

Perl

```perl
#!/usr/bin/perl -w
use strict;

my $html = $ARGV[0];

if ( $html =~ /\<[^\/>]+\ssummary=['\"][^'\"]*?['\"][^\/>]*\/?\>/ )
{
    print "Found match in '" . $html . "'\n";
}
else
{
    print "Didn't find match in string '" . $html . "'\n";
}
```

How It Works

This expression, when broken down, is as follows:

\<	a < to start out the HTML tag . . .
[^	a character class that doesn't contain . . .
\/	a slash . . .
>	or > . . .
]	the end of the character class . . .
+	found one or more times . . .
\s	whitespace . . .
summary	an *s*, *u*, *m*, *m*, *a*, *r*, and *y* . . .
=	an equal sign . . .
['\"]	either single or double quote . . .
[^'\"]	a character class that isn't a single quote or a double quote . . .

*?	found none, once, or many times with a lazy qualifier ...
['\"]	a double quote ...
[^	a character class that matches anything except ...
\/	a slash ...
>	the end of the HTML tag ...
]	the end of the character class ...
*?	none, once, or many times, up to ...
\/	a slash ...
\>	the end of the HTML tag.

This will find any tag that contains a summary attribute and will ignore anything that doesn't appear to be inside an HTML tag.

PHP

```
<html>
<head><title>5-5 Searching for HTML attributes</title></head>
<body>
<form action="recipe5-5.php" method="post">
<input type="text" name="str"
    value="<?php print htmlspecialchars( $_POST['str'] );?>" /><br />
<input type="submit" value="Find summary attribute" /><br /><br />
<?php
if ( $_SERVER['REQUEST_METHOD'] == "POST" )
{
    $str = $_POST['str'];
    if ( preg_match( "/(?:\<[^\/>]+\ssummary=['\"][^'\"]*?['\"][^\/>]*?\/?\>)/",
        $str ) )
    {
        print "<b>Found match in text:  '" . htmlspecialchars($str) .
            "'</b><br/>";
    }
    else
    {
        print "<b>Match not found in text:  '" . htmlspecialchars($str) .
            "'</b><br/>";
    }
}
?>
</form>
</body>
</html>
```

How It Works

To read more about this expression, see "How It Works" under the Perl example.

Shell Scripting

```
$ grep -e '<[^\/>]\+[[:space:]]summary=[\'"][^\'"]*[\'"]' filename
```

How It Works

See "How It Works" under the Perl example for a breakdown of a similar expression. The most notable difference is the [[:space:]] character class instead of Perl's \s.

Vim

```
/<[^\/>]\+\ssummary=['\"][^'\"]*['\"][^\/>]*\/\?>
```

How It Works

To see a breakdown of this expression, refer to "How It Works" under the Perl example. This expression is identical to the Perl expression with the exception of the double quotes and question mark being escaped.

5-6. Escaping Characters for HTML

This recipe shows an example of replacing > with < but makes sure that it isn't a part of an HTML tag. The string <p> replace > this </p> is replaced with <p> replace < this </p>.

Perl

```perl
#!/usr/bin/perl -w
use strict;

my $fn = $ARGV[0] || die "Please supply a parameter!\n";

open( FILE, $fn ) || die "Cannot open file!\n";

while ( <FILE> )
{
    my $line = reverse $_;
    $line =~ s/>(?![^><]+?\/?<)/;tl&/g;
    $line = reverse $line;
    print $line;
}

close( FILE );
```

How It Works

This one was a little tricky to put together, because in the recipe I needed to make sure the > character wasn't the closing of an HTML tag. Without using back references to put the strings back into the replacements, I was limited to using look-behinds. However, many implementations of regular expressions, including Perl and PHP, don't support variable-length look-behinds. Since I didn't know how long an HTML tag could be, I needed to have variable-length capability.

So I cheated. Just a little. In this recipe, I used the languages' capabilities (Perl, PHP) to reverse the string, and then I attacked it with an expression this time looking *ahead* to make sure the character is after a full tag.

The group in this expression matches everything from the beginning of an HTML tag up to a > that isn't inside an HTML tag. Broken down, the expression is as follows:

>	a > sign . . .
(?!	a negative look-ahead that contains . . .
[^	a character class that *doesn't* include . . .
>	a > . . .
<	or < . . .
+?	found one or more times, but matching as little as possible . . .

\/   a / (escaped for Perl) . . .

?   found zero or one time . . .

<   a < . . .

)   the end of the look-ahead.

PHP

```
<html>
<head><title>5-6 Escaping characters for HTML</title></head>
<body>
<form action="recipe5-6.php" method="post">
<input type="text" name="html"
    value="<?php print $_POST['html'];?>" /><br />
<input type="submit" value="Escape (not from Alcatraz)" /><br /><br />
<?php
if ( $_SERVER['REQUEST_METHOD'] == "POST" )
{
    $html = $_POST['html'];
    print "<b>Original text was:  '" . htmlspecialchars($html) . "'</b><br/>";
    $html = strrev( $html );
    $newhtml = preg_replace( "/>(?![^><]+?\/?<)/", ";tl&", $html );
    $newhtml = strrev( $newhtml );
    print "<b>New text is:  '" . htmlspecialchars($newhtml) . "'</b><br/>";
}
?>
</form>
</body>
</html>
```

How It Works

Refer to "How It Works" under the Perl example to see this expression explained.

5-7. Finding Unclosed XML Tags

This expression will allow you to find unclosed XML tags. It will match strings such as
`<myxml></myxml>` but fail on `<myxml><myxml>`.

Perl

```perl
#!/usr/bin/perl -w
use strict;

my $xml = $ARGV[0];

if ( $xml =~ /\<([^> \/]+)[^>]*?\>(?:.*?)\<\/\1\>/ )
{
        print "Looks good!  Original input is:  '" . $xml . "'\n";
}
else
{
        print "Suspect unclosed XML tag in '" . $xml . "'\n";
}
```

How It Works

This recipe works by using \1 in the search expression to make sure the closing tag has the
same text as the opening tag. It breaks down into the following:

\<	a < to open the XML tag ...
(	a capturing group that contains ...
[^	a character class that isn't ...
>	a > ...
<space>	a space ...
\/	a / ...
]	the end of the character class ...
+	one time or more ...
)	the end of the capturing group ...
[^	another character class that doesn't contain ...
>	a > ...
]	the end of the character class ...
*?	none, once, or many times up to ...
\>	the close of the XML tag ...

HTML AND XML

(?;	a noncapturing group that contains . . .
.	any character . . .
*?	found none, one, or many times . . .
)	the end of the noncapturing group . . .
\<	the beginning of the matching XML tag . . .
\/	an escaped / . . .
\1	the group matched with ([^> \/]+), which will be the XML tag name . . .
\>	the close of the ending XML tag.

This expression will match a string that has a closing and ending tag. One limitation of the expression as it's shown here is that it doesn't find nested XML tags. This is something you must overcome by using the features of the programming language.

PHP

```
<html>
<head><title>5-7 Finding unclosed XML tags</title></head>
<body>
<form action="recipe5-7.php" method="post">
<input type="text" name="str"
    value="<?php print $_POST['str'];?>" /><br />
<input type="submit" value="Find unclosed tags" /><br /><br />
<?php
if ( $_SERVER['REQUEST_METHOD'] == "POST" )
{
    $str = $_POST['str'];
    if ( preg_match( "/\<([^> \/]+)[^>]*?\>(?:.*?)\<\/\\1\>/", $str ) )
    {
        print "<b>XML looks good:  '" . htmlspecialchars($str) .
            "'</b><br/>";
    } else {
    print "<b>Bad XML!!  Bad!!!:  '" . htmlspecialchars($str) .
        "'</b><br/>";
    }
}
?>
</form>
</body>
</html>
```

How It Works

To read about how this expression works, refer to "How It Works" under the Perl example in this recipe.

See Also 1-10, 1-11

CHAPTER 6

■■■

Coding and Using Commands

This chapter includes recipes that you can use while writing software in C, C++, and Java and also while performing system administration tasks. Since the focus of this book is on open-source technologies, the system administration tasks are tailored for Linux operating systems. Most will be very close to Berkeley Software Distribution (BSD) operating systems such as FreeBSD and Mac OS X.

Caution In some of the recipes, I change method names and perform some other tasks that could be used for some light refactoring. Regular expressions can come in handy, but they aren't a substitute for getting the code right the first time.

6-1. Finding Code Comments

You can use this recipe to find comments in code. It will match C, C++, Java-style, and single-line comments, and it will also ignore comments in double quotes. Matches are `/* comment here*/` and `// comment here` but not `"/* this is not a comment */"` (in quotes).

Perl

```
#!/usr/bin/perl -w
use strict;

open ( FILE, $ARGV[0] ) || die "Cannot open file!";
while (<FILE>)
{
    my $line = $_;
    print $line if ( $line =~
        /^(?:[^"]*?(?:"[^"]*?"[^"]*?)?)*(?:\/\*|\/\/)/ );
}

close( FILE );
```

How It Works

The first part of this expression, `^(?:[^"]*?(?:"[^"]*?"[^"]*?)?)*`, makes sure the comment that's matched isn't inside quotes. It does this by making sure an even number of quotes appear before what could be a comment. If it finds an odd number of quotes before the start of the comment, you can assume that the code is in comments. One issue with this expression is that it doesn't deal with escaped quotes on a line, so beware that escaped quotes such as \" will cause the comment to be undetected if the escaped quotes aren't matched. The following example will cause the comment to be ignored:

```
"I have a double quote: \"" /*This is my ignored comment */
```

Of course, this doesn't take into account quotes spanning more than one line; if you think this is the case in your data, you can use the multiline option in regular expressions to span lines. See the "Syntax Overview" section in this book for more information about using the multiline option for searches in Perl.

This first part breaks down as follows:

^	the beginning of the line . . .
(?:	a noncapturing group that contains . . .
[^	a character class that isn't . . .
"	a double quote . . .
]	the end of the character class . . .
*?	found zero, one, or many times up to . . .

(?:	another noncapturing group that contains . . .
"	a double quote . . .
[^	a character class that isn't . . .
"	a double quote . . .
]	the end of the character class . . .
*?	found zero, one, or many times . . .
"	a double quote, followed by . . .
[^	a character class that doesn't match . . .
"	another double quote . . .
]	the end of the character class . . .
*?	zero, one, or many times . . .
)	the end of the noncapturing group . . .
?	where the whole group appears at most once . . .
)	the end of the outer noncapturing group . . .
*	found zero, one, or many times.

So this expression is making sure that if a double quote is found, it's followed by one more that isn't followed by another one. (Thus, you get an even number of quotes.) You can use this expression to start any other expression where you want to make sure it matches something that isn't inside quotes.

The second part of the expression is pretty straightforward and matches the comment itself. Here all you care about finding is the beginning of the comment—it doesn't matter what's inside it or how it ends at this point. All you know is that you've found the beginning of a comment that isn't in quotes—which is good enough for this search. The comment expression is as follows:

(?:	a noncapturing group that contains . . .
\/	a slash . . .
*	an asterisk . . .
|	or . . .
\/	a slash . . .
\/	another slash . . .
)	the end of a group.

This will match strings that start with /* or //.

PHP

```
<html>
<head><title>6-1 Finding code comments</title></head>
<body>
<form action="recipe6-1.php" method="post">
<input type="text" name="str"
value="<?php print $_POST['str'];?>" /><br />
<input type="submit" value="Find comments" /><br /><br />
<?php
if ( $_SERVER['REQUEST_METHOD'] == "POST" )
{
$str = $_POST['str'];
    if ( preg_match( "/^(?:[^\"]*?(?:\"[^\"]*?\"[^\"]*?)?)*(?:\/\*|\/\/)/",
        $str ) )
    {
        print "<b>Found comment in text:  '" .
        htmlspecialchars($str) . "'</b><br/>";
    }
    else
    {
        print "<b>Did NOT find comment in text:  '" .
        htmlspecialchars($str) . "'</b><br/>";
    }
}
?>
</form>
</body>
</html>
```

How It Works

I explain this example, which uses Perl-Compatible Regular Expressions (PCREs), in the "How It Works" section under the Perl example in this recipe. The previous PHP example has the same limitations as the Perl example.

Shell Scripting

```
$ grep -e '^\([^"]*\("[^"]*"[^"]*\)\?\)*\(/\/*\|\/\/\)' filename
```

How It Works

The grep recipe has the same limitations as the others when it comes to escaped double quotes; the assumption with this expression is that they will be closed when inside a set of double quotes.

Note The grep recipe doesn't have the ability to do multiline searches.

The following is a breakdown of the grep recipe shown previously:

^	the beginning of the line . . .
\(	a group that contains . . .
[^"]	a character class that doesn't contain a double quote . . .
*	zero, one, or many times . . .
\(	a group that contains . . .
"	a double quote . . .
[^"]	a character class that doesn't contain a double quote . . .
*	zero, one, or many times . . .
"	another double quote . . .
[^"]	a character class that doesn't contain another double quote . . .
*	zero, one, or many times . . .
\)	the end of the group . . .
\?	occurring at most once . . .
\)	the end of the group . . .
*	zero, one, or many times.

The previous expression makes sure that no unclosed double quotes appear before the comment, which ensures the comment isn't in quotes. The following expression will look for the actual comment opening:

\(	a group that contains . . .
\/	a slash . . .
*	a literal asterisk . . .
|	or . . .
\/	a slash . . .
\/	another slash . . .
\)	the end of the group.

This matches /* or //.

Vim

`/^\%([^"]\{-}\%("[^"]\{-}"[^"]*\)\?\)\?\%(\/\*\|\/\/\)`

How It Works

The `\{-}` combination is a lazy (or conservative) qualifier that matches as little as possible. I use it here so that the match stops at the first occurrence of another quote in the expression `\%([^"]\{-}\%("[^"]\{-}"[^"]\{-}\)\?\)\?`, which makes sure that the comment found isn't inside an open quote by making sure an even number of quotes appears before the opening of the comment.

Like the grep recipe, the previous Vim recipe doesn't have the ability to do multiline searches.

The following is a breakdown of this expression:

`^`	the beginning of the line . . .
`\%(`	a noncapturing group that contains . . .
`[^"]`	a character class that doesn't match a double quote . . .
`\{-}`	a lazy qualifier, that matches up to the next . . .
`\%(`	noncapturing group that contains . . .
`"`	a double quote . . .
`[^"]`	a character class that doesn't contain a double quote . . .
`\{-}`	found as many times as necessary, up to the first . . .
`"`	double quote . . .
`[^"]`	a character class that doesn't match a double quote . . .
`*`	found zero, one, or many times . . .
`\)`	the end of the noncapturing group . . .
`\?`	found at most one time . . .
`\)`	the end of the outer noncapturing group . . .
`\?`	found at most one time.

Once this expression makes sure that no unclosed quote precedes the beginning of the comment, it's up to the next expression to search for the beginning of a comment. All it cares about is the opening, so it looks for `//` or `/*`. (There's no need to make sure it's closed with `*/`.) The expression is `\%(\/\*\|\/\/\)`, which breaks down as follows:

\%(	a noncapturing group that contains . . .
\/	a slash . . .
*	a literal star . . .
|	or . . .
\/	a slash . . .
\/	followed by another slash . . .
\)	the end of the group.

This will match either /* or //.

See Also 3-4, 3-6, 6-8, 6-9

6-2. Finding Lines with an Odd Number of Quotes

This recipe looks for lines with an odd number of quotes in a single line. I've found it incredibly useful to narrow down quote issues in shell scripts when syntax highlighting wasn't available to help me find unclosed quotes. This recipe will match the strings Unclosed, which has an unclosed double quote, and \"this", which has an odd number of quotes.

This expression assumes it doesn't matter whether the quotes are escaped; it assumes only that an odd number of them is an issue.

Perl

```
#!/usr/bin/perl -w
use strict;

open ( FILE, $ARGV[0] ) || die "Cannot open file!";
while (<FILE>)
{
    my $line = $_;
    print $line if ( $line =~ /^[^"]*"([^"]*|([^"]*"[^"]*"[^"]*)*)$/ );
}

close( FILE );
```

How It Works

It's best to go through this expression by breaking it down into a few parts. Overall, the purpose of the expression is to find a quote, and when it does, it makes sure the quote either isn't followed by another one at all or is followed by an even number of quotes. If it's the only one on the line, you'll assume it's mismatched. If it's followed by an even number of quotes, it's also mismatched because an odd number of them appear on the line.

Make sure the quote is found on a line with no other quote before it. (You want to start with a clean slate.) The expression breaks down as follows:

    ^   the beginning of the line . . .

    [^"]   a character class that doesn't match a double quote . . .

    *   found zero or more times . . .

    "   a double quote.

The group that follows this part of the expression has two parts separated by the or operator |.

    [^"]   a character class that doesn't match a double quote . . .

    *   found zero or more times.

Finally, the expression ([^"]*"[^"]*"[^"]*)* will look for an even number of quotes by saying the following:

(a group that contains . . .

[^"]   a character class that isn't a quote . . .

*   found zero or more times . . .

"   a quote . . .

[^"]   a character class that isn't a quote . . .

*   found zero or more times (so the quote isn't closed) . . .

"   a quote . . .

[^"]   a character class that isn't a quote . . .

*   found zero or more times . . .

)   the end of the group . . .

*   where the group can repeat (this allows even numbers).

PHP

```
<html>
<head><title>6-2 Finding mismatched quotes</title></head>
<body>
<form action="recipe6-2.php" method="post">
<input type="text" name="str"
    value="<?php print $_POST['str'];?>" /><br />
<input type="submit" value="Find mismatched quotes" /><br /><br />
<?php
if ( $_SERVER['REQUEST_METHOD'] == "POST" )
{
    $str = $_POST['str'];
    if ( preg_match( "/^[^"]*"([^"]*|([^"]*"[^"]*"[^"]*)*)$/", $str ) )
    {
        print "<b>Found mismatched quotes in text:  '" .
            htmlspecialchars($str) . "'</b><br/>";
    }
    else
    {
        print "<b>Found matched quotes in text:  '" .
            htmlspecialchars($str) . "'</b><br/>";
    }
```

```
}
?>
</form>
</body>
</html>
```

How It Works

I detail this expression under "How It Works" in the Perl example. The PHP example requires double quotes to be escaped here, but otherwise it's identical to the Perl example.

Shell Scripting

```
$ grep '^[^"]*"\([^"]*\|\([^"]*"[^"]*"[^"]*\)*\)*)$' filename
```

How It Works

See "How It Works" under the Perl example, and remember to escape (,), and |.

Vim

```
/^[^"]*"\([^"]*\|\([^"]*"[^"]*"[^"]*\)*\)*)$
```

How It Works

See "How It Works" under the Perl example in this expression.

See Also 3-1, 3-2, 3-4, 6-1

6-3. Reordering Method Parameters

You can use this recipe to change the order of parameters in a method.

```
MyMethod( 1, "mystring" )
```

becomes

```
MyMethod( "mystring", 1 )
```

In this case, MyMethod has only two parameters.

Perl

```perl
#!/usr/bin/perl -w
use strict;

open ( FILE, $ARGV[0] ) || die "Cannot open file!";
while (<FILE>)
{
    my $line = $_;
    $line =~ s/MyMethod\s*\(\s*(\"?\w+\"?)\s*,\s*(\"?\w+\"?)\s*\)\s*;↵
/MyMethod( $2, $1 );/g;
    print $line;
}

close( FILE );
```

How It Works

For brevity, I'll break down the expression starting after MyMethod.

\s	whitespace . . .
*	zero, one, or many times . . .
\(	a literal parenthesis . . .
\s	whitespace . . .
*	zero, one, or many times . . .
(	a group that will capture . . .
\"	a double quote . . .
?	that can occur at most once . . .
\w	a word character . . .
+	found one or more times . . .
\"	a double quote . . .

)   the end of the capturing group . . .

,   a comma . . .

\s   whitespace . . .

*   zero, one, or many times . . .

(a group that will capture . . .

\"   a double quote . . .

?   that can occur at most once . . .

\w   a word character . . .

+   found one or more times . . .

\"   a double quote . . .

)   the end of the capturing group . . .

\s   whitespace . . .

*   zero, one, or many times . . .

\)   a closing parenthesis . . .

;   a semicolon.

The first and second groups are captured and put back into the replacement string with the back references $1 and $2.

PHP

```
<html>
<head><title>6-3 Re-ordering method parameters</title></head>
<body>
<form action="recipe6-3.php" method="post">
<input type="text" name="str"
value="<?php print $_POST['str'];?>" /><br />
<input type="submit" value="Re-order parameters" /><br /><br />
<?php
if ( $_SERVER['REQUEST_METHOD'] == "POST" )
{
    $str = $_POST['str'];
    $newstr = preg_replace( "/MyMethod\s*\(\s*(\"?\w+\"?)\s*,↵
\s*(\"?\w+\"?)\s*\)\s*;/", "MyMethod( $2, $1 )", $str );
    print "<b>Original text was:  '" .
        htmlspecialchars($str) . "'</b><br/>";
    print "<b>New text is:  '" . htmlspecialchars($newstr) . "'</b><br/>";
}
```

```
?>
</form>
</body>
</html>
```

How It Works

Look at "How It Works" under the Perl example to see details about this expression.

Shell Scripting

```
$ sed 's/MyMethod *( *\(.*\), *\(.*\) *) *;/MyMethod( \2, \1 );/g' filename
```

How It Works

The sed expression shown here breaks down as follows:

<space>	a space . . .
*	zero, one, or more times . . .
(	a literal parenthesis . . .
<space>	a space . . .
*	zero or more times . . .
\(	a group that captures . . .
.	any character . . .
*	zero or more times, up to . . .
\)	the end of the capturing group . . .
,	a comma . . .
<space>	a space . . .
*	zero or more times . . .
\(. . .\)	a second group that captures the same thing as the first group . . .
<space>	a space . . .
*	zero or more times . . .
)	a literal parenthesis . . .
<space>	a space . . .
*	zero or more times . . .
;	the semicolon.

Vim

`:%s/MyMethod\s*(\s*\(.*\),\s*\(.*\)\s*)\s*;/MyMethod( \2, \1 );/g`

How It Works

Other than the use of \s to represent whitespace, this expression is identical to the one in the "Shell Scripting" section for this recipe.

■**See Also** 6-15

6-4. Changing a Method Name

You can use this recipe to change the name of a method in source code. MyMethod becomes MyNewMethod. This recipe assumes that comments aren't found within the MyMethod call, which is unlikely but possible.

Perl

```
#!/usr/bin/perl -w
use strict;

open ( FILE, $ARGV[0] ) || die "Cannot open file!";
while (<FILE>)
{
    my $line = $_;
    $line =~ s/\bMyMethod\s*\(/MyNewMethod(/g;
    print $line;
}

close( FILE );
```

How It Works

This expression simply looks for the method name, making sure it's a new word (so it doesn't mistakenly match something such as YourAndMyMethod).

\b	a word boundary ...
...	the method name ...
\s	whitespace ...
*	found zero or more times ...
\(	an open parenthesis.

PHP

```
<html>
<head><title>6-4 Changing a method name</title></head>
<body>
<form action="recipe6-4.php" method="post">
<input type="text" name="str"
value="<?php print $_POST['str'];?>" /><br />
<input type="submit" value="Change method name" /><br /><br />
<?php
if ( $_SERVER['REQUEST_METHOD'] == "POST" )
{
```

```
    $str = $_POST['str'];
    $newstr = preg_replace( "/\bMyMethod\s*\(/", "MyNewMethod(", $str );
    print "<b>Original text was:  '" .
        htmlspecialchars($str) . "'</b><br/>";
    print "<b>New text is:  '" . htmlspecialchars($newstr) . "'</b><br/>";
}
?>
</form>
</body>
</html>
```

How It Works

To read about this expression, see "How It Works" under the Perl example.

Shell Scripting

```
$ sed 's/\<MyMethod[[:space:]]*(/MyNewMethod (/g' filename
```

How It Works

The sed command replaces the MyMethod method with MyNewMethod. Instead of using a word anchor such as \b in PCRE, the sed example uses the expression \<, which is a word anchor as well. The other difference is the use of [[:space:]], which is a character class that matches whitespace in Portable Operating System Interface (POSIX) expressions.

Vim

```
:%s/\<MyMethod\s*(/MyNewMethod (/g
```

How It Works

The Vim search expression breaks down as follows:

\<	the beginning of a word . . .
. . .	the method name . . .
\s	whitespace . . .
*	found zero or more times . . .
(	an opening parenthesis.

6-5. Removing Inline Comments

This recipe allows you to remove inline, C-style comments that start with /* and end with */. The string int i = 0; /*define i here */ becomes int i = 0;.

Perl

```
#!/usr/bin/perl -w
use strict;

open ( FILE, $ARGV[0] ) || die "Cannot open file!";
while (<FILE>)
{
    my $line = $_;
    $line =~ s/\/\*.*?\*\///g;
    print $line;
}

close( FILE );
```

How It Works

The expression uses a lazy qualifier, *?, to match as little as possible. The expression matches the following:

\/	a slash . . .
*	a literal asterisk . . .
.	any character . . .
*?	found zero, one, or many times matching as little as possible . . .
*	a literal asterisk starting the close of the comment . . .
\/	a closing slash.

This allows a comment to be replaced by a zero-length string, which removes the comment from the line.

PHP

```
<html>
<head><title>6-5 Removing inline comments</title></head>
<body>
<form action="recipe6-5.php" method="post">
<input type="text" name="str"
value="<?php print $_POST['str'];?>" /><br />
<input type="submit" value="Remove inline comment" /><br /><br />
```

```php
<?php
if ( $_SERVER['REQUEST_METHOD'] == "POST" )
{
$str = $_POST['str'];
$newstr = preg_replace( "/\/\*.*?\*\//", "", $str );
print "<b>Original text was:  '" . htmlspecialchars($str) . "'</b><br/>";
print "<b>New text is:  '" . htmlspecialchars($newstr) . "'</b><br/>";
}
?>
</form>
</body>
</html>
```

How It Works

See "How It Works" under the Perl example of this recipe.

See Also 6-1, 6-8, 6-9

6-6. Commenting Out Code

This simple expression comments out code by replacing the beginning of the line with comments. It's most useful in editors that allow regular expressions to be used.

Perl

```perl
#!/usr/bin/perl -w
use strict;

my $fn = $ARGV[0] || die "Please supply a filename!";
open ( FILE, $ARGV[0] ) || die "Cannot open file.";

while (<FILE>)
{
    my $line = $_;
    $line =~ s/^/\/\/ /g;
    print $line;
}

close( FILE );
```

How It Works

The expression is simply ^, which is a line anchor that matches the beginning of the line but doesn't swallow any characters. The replacement expression is \/\/ , which adds two forward slashes and a space to the beginning of each line.

PHP

```php
<html>
<head><title>6-6 Commenting out code</title></head>
<body>
<form action="recipe6-6.php" method="post">
<textarea cols="20" rows="10" name="str"></textarea><br />
<input type="submit" value="Comment out code" /><br /><br />
<?php
if ( $_SERVER['REQUEST_METHOD'] == "POST" )
{
    $lines = explode( "\n", $_POST['str'] );
    foreach ( $lines as $line )
    {
        $newstr = preg_replace( "/^/", "// ", $line );
        print "<b>$newstr</b><br/>";
    }
```

```
}
?>
</form>
</body>
</html>
```

How It Works

See "How It Works" under the Perl example.

Shell Scripting

```
$ sed 's/^/\/\///' filename
```

How It Works

See "How it Works" under the Perl example for an explanation of this expression.

Vim

```
:%s/^/\/\//
```

How It Works

See "How It Works" under the Perl example in this recipe for a walk-through of this expression.

■**See Also** 1-21, 6-7

6-7. Uncommenting Out Code

This recipe will remove the comments by removing the // from the beginning of the lines in a file. It's important to think about this a little bit before running it on your file—it may remove comments from lines you still want commented out.

Perl

```perl
#!/usr/bin/perl -w
use strict;

my $fn = $ARGV[0] || die "Please supply a filename!";
open ( FILE, $ARGV[0] ) || die "Cannot open file.";

while (<FILE>)
{
    my $line = $_;
    $line =~ s/^\/\/ //g;
    print $line;
}

close( FILE );
```

How It Works

This expression matches the following:

^	the beginning of the line . . .
\/	a slash . . .
\/	another slash . . .
<space>	a space.

This is replaced with a zero-length string, which will remove it from the line. Nothing happens to the ^; it's simply a line anchor that matches the beginning of the line without matching any real characters.

PHP

```php
<html>
<head><title>6-7 Uncommenting out code</title></head>
<body>
<form action="recipe6-7.php" method="post">
<textarea cols="20" rows="10" name="str"></textarea><br />
<input type="submit" value="Uncommenting out code" /><br /><br />
<?php
```

```php
if ( $_SERVER['REQUEST_METHOD'] == "POST" )
{
    $lines = explode( "\n", $_POST['str'] );
    foreach ( $lines as $line )
    {
        $newstr = preg_replace( "/^\/\/ /", "", $line );
        print "<b>$newstr</b><br/>";
    }
}
?>
</form>
</body>
</html>
```

How It Works

See "How It Works" under the Perl example for an explanation of this expression.

Shell Scripting

```
$ sed 's/^\/\///' filename
```

How It Works

See "How It Works" under the Perl example in this recipe for an explanation of this expression.

Vim

```
:%s/^\/\///
```

How It Works

For an explanation of this expression, see the Perl example in this recipe.

See Also 1-21, 6-7

6-8. Searching for Variable Declarations

This recipe allows you to search for a variable declaration. This expression is smart enough to look for a declaration that isn't in comments. The declaration that's searched for in this example is int myvar—you don't know whether it's public or private, so the expression looks for either one.

Note This expression was tested specifically on Java and C++ code.

Perl

```perl
#!/usr/bin/perl -w
use strict;

my $fn = $ARGV[0] || die "Please supply a filename!";
open ( FILE, $ARGV[0] ) || die "Cannot open file.";

while (<FILE>)
{
    my $line = $_;
    print $line if ( $line =~
/^(?:(?:(?!\/\/|\/\*).)*|(?:(?!\/\*).)*\/\*.*?\*\/(?:(?!\/\*).)*)(public|private)?↵
\s+int\s+myvar\s+=/
);
}

close( FILE );
```

How It Works

The bulk of this expression makes sure the declaration isn't found inside a comment. This part of the expression is ^(?:(?:(?!\/\/|\/*).)*|(?:(?!\/*).)*\/*.*?*\/(?:(?!\/*).)*), which I'll break into smaller parts so you can digest it a little easier. It consists of two parts separated by the or operator |. The first part is (?:(?!\/\/|\/*).)*, and the second is (?:(?!\/*).)*\/*.*?*\/(?:(?!\/*).)*).

Note Multiline variable declarations aren't included in the results of this expression.

The first group makes sure the line doesn't have // or /* somewhere before the declaration. The second group says, "If it does have /* before it, make sure there's */ somewhere after it and not another opening comment." The first group breaks down as follows:

(?:	a noncapturing group that contains . . .
(?!	a negative look-ahead with . . .
\/\/	two slashes . . .
|	or . . .
\/*	a slash and a literal asterisk . . .
)	the end of the negative look-ahead . . .
.	any character . . .
)	the end of the noncapturing group . . .
*	found zero, one, or many times.

This expression will make sure the line doesn't contain // or /* in front of the declaration. The second group, separated by the or operator |, makes sure that if a /* sequence is found that it ends with a */ sequence before the declaration and that no other /* sequence if found again before the declaration. The following is that expression, broken down:

(?:	a noncapturing group that contains . . .
(?!	a negative look-ahead with . . .
\/*	a /* combination . . .
)	the end of the negative look-ahead . . .
.	any character . . .
)	the end of the noncapturing group . . .
*	zero, one, or many times . . .
\/*	a comment opening /* . . .
.	any character . . .
*?	found zero, one, or many times (but as few as possible) . . .
*\/	a */ combination . . .
(?:	a noncapturing group . . .
(?!	a negative look-ahead . . .
\/*	a /* combination . . .
)	the end of the negative look-ahead . . .
.	any character . . .
)	the end of the noncapturing group . . .

*	zero, one, or many times . . .
)	the end of the noncapturing group.

After you're sure the declaration isn't found inside comments, you can search for the declaration.

(	a group that contains . . .
public	the characters $p, u, b, l, i,$ and c . . .
|	or . . .
private	the characters p, r, i, v, a, t, e . . .
)	the end of the group . . .
\s	whitespace . . .
+	found one or many times . . .
int	i, n, t . . .
\s	whitespace . . .
+	found one or many times . . .
myvar	the variable name . . .
\s	whitespace . . .
+	found one or more times . . .
=	equal sign.

This is all the expression cares about for the variable declaration—it knows enough at this point to tell that a variable is being declared and set to something.

PHP

```
<html>
<head><title>6-8 Searching for variable declarations</title></head>
<body>
<form action="recipe6-8.php" method="post">
<input type="text" name="str"
    value="<?php print $_POST['str'];?>" /><br />
<input type="submit" value="Find variable declarations" /><br /><br />
<?php
if ( $_SERVER['REQUEST_METHOD'] == "POST" )
{
    $str = $_POST['str'];
    if ( preg_match( "/^(?:(?:(?!\/\/|\/\*).)*| ↵
```

```
(?:(?!\/\*).)*\/\*.*?\*\/(?:(?!\/\*).)*)(public|private)? ↩
\s+int\s+myvar\s+=/
", $str ) )
    {
    print "<b>Found declaration in:  '" .
        htmlspecialchars($str) . "'</b><br/>";
    }
    else
    {
        print "<b>Found no match in text:  '" .
            htmlspecialchars($str) . "'</b><br/>";
    }
}
?>
</form>
</body>
</html>
```

How It Works

See "How It Works" under the Perl example for an explanation of this recipe.

Vim

```
/^\(\(\(\(\/\/\|\/\*\)\@!.\)*\|\(\(\/\*\)\@!.\)*\/\*.*\*\/\(\(\/\*\)\@!.\)*\) ↩
\(public\|private\)\?\s\+int\s\+myvar\s\+=
```

How It Works

This expression is a modified version of the PCRE expression with added escapes before the (,), +, and |. Also, the (?! negative look-ahead is replaced by the Vim \@! that *follows* the expression that it modifies.

■ **See Also** 1-3, 1-19, 6-8

6-9. Searching for Words Within Comments

You can use this recipe to search for a word in code and to make sure the word is found within comments. The string // WORD will match on a line and so will /* WORD */.

Perl

```perl
#!/usr/bin/perl -w
use strict;

open ( FILE, $ARGV[0] ) || die "Cannot open file!";
while (<FILE>)
{
    my $line = $_;
    if ( $line =~ /^(?:\/\*(?:(?!\*\/).)*|\/\/.*?)WORD/ )
    {
        print $line;
    }
}

close( FILE );
```

How It Works

The previous recipe, recipe 6-8, focused on making sure a search string wasn't in comments. This expression does the opposite—it makes sure that any comment that's opened isn't closed before the word, or it makes sure that the line comment // is before the word. The following are the details:

^	the beginning of the line . . .
(?:	a noncapturing group that contains . . .
\/*	the opening of a comment . . .
(?:	a noncapturing group . . .
(?!	a negative look-ahead . . .
*\/	the closing of the comment . . .
)	the end of the negative look-ahead . . .
.	any character . . .
)	the end of the noncapturing group . . .
*	zero, one, or many times . . .
|	or . . .
\/\/	a line comment // . . .

.   any character . . .

*?   a lazy qualifier that matches as little as possible . . .

)   the end of the outer noncapturing group . . .

WORD   up to the word you're trying to find.

Substitute WORD with the word you're looking for inside comments.

▪**Note** For brevity, I didn't include word anchors in this expression so the text WORD will be matched in this expression. It will find SWORD and PASSWORD as well as WORDS and WORDSMITH. To look for a whole word, combine this recipe with recipe 1-2.

PHP

```
<html>
<head><title>6-9 Searching for words within comments</title></head>
<body>
<form action="recipe6-9.php" method="post">
<input type="text" name="str"
value="<?php print $_POST['str'];?>" /><br />
<input type="submit" value="Find WORD in comments" /><br /><br />
<?php
if ( $_SERVER['REQUEST_METHOD'] == "POST" )
{
    $str = $_POST['str'];
    if ( preg_match( "/^(?:\/\*(?:(?!\*\/).)*|\/\/.*?)WORD/", $str ) )
    {
        print "<b>Found WORD in comments:  '" . htmlspecialchars($str)
            .."'</b><br/>";
    }
    else
    {
        print "<b>Found no match in text:  '" .
            htmlspecialchars($str) . "'</b><br/>";
    }
}
?>
</form>
</body>
</html>
```

How It Works

See "How It Works" under the Perl example for an explanation of this expression.

Vim

```
/^\(\/\*\(\(\(\*\/\)\@!.\)*\|\/\/.*\)WORD
```

How It Works

This expression uses the Vim \@! notation for a negative look-ahead. It makes sure the sequence *\ isn't found between the opening /* and the characters WORD.

■**See Also** 1-3, 1-19, 6-8

6-10. Filtering the Output of ps

You can use this recipe to filter the output of ps for a slightly friendlier format. It will make this line

```
root      81   0.0  0.0     18092    208  ??  Ss     Thu09AM   0:00.66↵
/usr/sbin/syslogd -s -m 0
```

look like the following:

```
81:/usr/sbin/syslogd (root)
```

Perl

```
#!/usr/bin/perl -w
use strict;

while (<STDIN>)
{
    print $_ if ( s/^(root)\s+(\d+)\s+.*\s+(\/.*syslogd)(?:\s+-?\w+)*$↵
/$2:$3 ($1)/ );
}
```

How It Works

This example looks specifically for the syslogd process run by the user root in the output of ps aux. When it finds the line, it reformats it. Variations on this expression could relax the searching a bit to reformat each line or to format and print lines from a certain user only.

The search expression is as follows:

^	the beginning of the line . . .
(	a group that captures . . .
root	r, o, o, and t . . .
)	the end of the group . . .
\s	whitespace . . .
+	found one or more times . . .
(	a second group that captures . . .
\d	a digit (for the process identifier) . . .
+	one or more times . . .
)	the end of the second group . . .
\s	whitespace . . .

+	found one or more times ...
.	any character ...
*	found zero, one, or many times ...
\s	whitespace ...
+	one or more times ...
(	a third group that captures ...
\/	a slash ...
.	any character ...
*	found zero, one, or many times, up to ...
syslogd	the syslogd process ...
)	the end of the group.

The last part of the expression, (?:\s+-?\w+)*$, matches parameters after the command name up to the end of the line. The expression breaks down as follows:

(?:	a noncapturing group that contains ...
\s	whitespace ...
+	that's found one or more times ...
-	a hyphen (dash) ...
?	that can be found zero or one time ...
\w	a word character ...
+	found one or more times ...
)	the end of the group ...
*	found zero or more times ...
$	the end of the line.

The three groups are put back into the replacement string in a format to be displayed in the output: $2:$3 ($1).

Python

```
#!/usr/bin/python
import re
from os import popen

output = popen( 'ps aux' )
regex = re.compile( r'^(root)\s+(\d+)\s+.*\s+(\/.*syslogd)(?:\s-?\w+)*$' )
lines = output.readlines()
for line in lines:
    if regex.match( line ):
        formatted = regex.sub( r'\2:\3 (\1)', line )
        print formatted,
output.close()
```

How It Works

This Python script reads the output of ps aux, sees if the line matches the regular expression, and, if it does, prints the formatted version of the line.

See "How It Works" under the Perl example for a full explanation of this expression.

6-11. Filtering the Output of netstat

This recipe will filter the output of netstat -p tcp into a friendly format. The lines

```
tcp4      0      0  localhost.netinfo-loca localhost.988           ESTABLISHED
tcp4      0      0  localhost.988            localhost.netinfo-loca ESTABLISHED
```

become the following:

```
Found established connection:  localhost.netinfo-loca -> localhost.988
Found established connection:  localhost.988 -> localhost.netinfo-loca
```

Perl

```perl
#!/usr/bin/perl -w
use strict;

while (<STDIN>)
{
    print $_ if ( s/^(?:.*\s+)([-\w.:]+)\s+([-\w.:]+)(?:\s+ESTABLISHED)/↵
Found established connection:  $1 -> $2/g );
}
```

How It Works

This Perl script takes input from STDIN and filters it for an established connection. If it finds one, it prints a formatted line.

The expression uses grouping to capture the source and destination hosts and the expression ESTABLISHED to format only established connections.

^	the beginning of the line ...
(?:	a noncapturing group that contains ...
.	any character ...
*	zero, one, or many times ...
\s	whitespace ...
+	one or many times ...
(	a group that contains ...
[	a character class with ...
-	a hyphen ...
\w	a word character class ...
.	a period (dot) ...
:	a colon ...

]	the end of the character class . . .
+	one or many times . . .
)	the end of the group . . .
\s	whitespace . . .
+	one or many times . . .
(	a group that contains . . .
[	a character class with . . .
-	a hyphen . . .
\w	a word character class . . .
.	a period (dot) . . .
:	a colon . . .
]	the end of the character class . . .
+	one or many times . . .
)	the end of the group . . .
(?:	a noncapturing group that contains . . .
\s	whitespace . . .
+	one or more times . . .
ESTABLISHED	to search for established connections . . .
)	the end of the group.

You could tweak this expression to be more exact in its matching, but one of the luxuries of formatting command output is that the output is very consistent—with the exceptions of tweaks to the regular expression to allow for different versions of a command. If this were user input you were parsing, the expression would have to be more exact. In other words, don't get wrapped up in making a very complicated expression if a simple one will do.

PHP

```
<html>
<head><title>6-11 Filtering the output of netstat</title></head>
<body>
<form action="recipe6-11.php" method="post">
<input type="submit" value="Run netstat" /><br /><br />
<?php
if ( $_SERVER ['REQUEST_METHOD'] == "POST" )
{
```

```php
$ps = popen( 'netstat -p tcp', 'r' );
while ( $buffer = fgets( $ps, 2056 ) )
{
    $output .= $buffer;
}

$lines = explode( "\n", $output );

foreach ( $lines as $line )
{
    if ( preg_match( "/^(?:.*\s+)([-\w.:]+)\s+([-\w.:]+)(?:\s+ESTABLISHED)/",
        $line ) )
    {
        $newstr = preg_replace( "/^(?:.*\s+)([-\w.:]+)\s+↵
([-\w.:]+)(?:\s+ESTABLISHED)/",
"Found established connection:  $1 -> $2", $line );
        print "<b>$newstr</b><br/>";
    }
}

    pclose($ps);
}
?>
</form>
</body>
</html>
```

How It Works

Upon submission, this PHP script runs the command and parses the output with the expression. To read about the expression used here, see the Perl example in this recipe.

Python

```python
#!/usr/bin/python
import re
from os import popen

output = popen( 'netstat -p tcp' )
regex = re.compile( r'^(?:.*\s+)([-\w.:]+)\s+([-\w.:]+)(?:\s+ESTABLISHED)' )
lines = output.readlines()
for line in lines:
    if regex.match( line ):
        formatted = regex.sub( r'Found established connection:  \1 -> \2', line )
        print formatted,
output.close()
```

How It Works

To see this expression explained in detail, refer to "How It Works" under the Perl example.

▪**See Also** 6-10, 6-12

6-12. Filtering the Output of du

This recipe filters the output of du to find directories that contain more than 200 megabytes (MB) of files.

Perl

```perl
#!/usr/bin/perl -w
use strict;

while (<STDIN>)
{
    print $_ if ( s/^(?:(?:[2-9][0-9]{2}M)|(?:[0-9.]+G))\s+(.*)$/↵
Directory larger than 200M: $1/g
);
}
```

How It Works

The command du -hs will print the summary of disk usage for directories. The -h command makes the output "human readable," which prints M for megabytes and K for kilobytes. This recipe uses ranges to filter the output to find and show directories larger than 200MB. It searches for any set of numbers that ends with G, which represents gigabytes, because any number of gigabytes will be larger than 200MB.

The expression is as follows:

^	the beginning of the line ...
(?:	a noncapturing group that contains ...
(?:	a noncapturing group that contains ...
[2-9]	a digit two through nine ...
[0-9]	a digit zero through nine ...
{2}	found two times ...
M	an M (printed by du -h for megabytes) ...
)	the end of the inside group ...
|	or ...
(?:	another noncapturing group that contains ...
[0-9.]	a character class that contains zero through nine or a literal ...
+	found one of more times ...
G	a G ...

)	the end of the group ...
)	the end of the outside group ...
\s	whitespace ...
+	one or more times ...
(	a group that contains ...
.	any character ...
*	found zero, one, or many times ...
$	the end of the line.

By tweaking the ranges (for instance, changing the first one to [5-9]), you can limit the output to different thresholds.

PHP

```php
<html>
<head><title>6-12 Filtering the output of du</title></head>
<body>
<form action="recipe6-12.php" method="post">
<input type="submit" value="Find big directory" /><br /><br />
<?php
if ( $_SERVER['REQUEST_METHOD'] == "POST" )
{
    $ps = popen( 'du -hs /', 'r' );
    while ( $stuff = fgets( $ps, 2056 ) )
    {
        $output .= $stuff;
    }

    $lines = explode( "\n", $output );

    foreach ( $lines as $line )
    {
        if ( preg_match( "/^(?:[2-9][0-9]{2}M)\s+(.*)$/", $line ) )
        {
            $newstr = preg_replace( "/^(?:(?:[2-9][0-9]{2}M)| ↩
(?:[0-9.]+G))\s+(.*)$/",
                "Directory larger than 200M:  $1", $line );
            print "<b>$newstr</b><br/>";
        }
    }
}
```

```
    pclose($ps);
}
?>
</form>
</body>
</html>
```

How It Works

See "How It Works" under the Perl example in this recipe for an explanation of this expression.

Python

```
#!/usr/bin/python
import re
from os import popen

output = popen( 'du -hs /home/myuser/*' )
regex = re.compile( r'^(?:(?:[2-9][0-9]{2}M)|(?:[0-9.]+G))\s+(.*)$' )

lines = output.readlines()
for line in lines:
    if regex.match( line ):
        formatted = regex.sub( r'You have more than 200MB in directory: \1', line )
        print formatted
output.close()
```

How It Works

Before running the Python example, replace /home/myuser/* with a directory on your system. See "How It Works" under the Perl example for a description of this expression.

6-13. Setting a SQL Owner

This handy recipe will insert an owner on stored procedures in a script where there's no owner. This can especially be useful in large scripts where you may have forgotten to assign an owner to the objects. It will not add an owner if there's already one assigned. The line

```
CREATE PROCEDURE MYPROC
```

becomes the following:

```
CREATE PROCEDURE [dbo].[MYPROC]
```

Perl

```perl
#!/usr/bin/perl -w
use strict;

open ( FILE, $ARGV[0] ) || die "Cannot open file!";

while (<FILE>)
{
    my $line = $_;
    $line =~ s/(CREATE\s+PROCEDURE\s+)(?!\[?\w+\]?\.)(\w+)/$1\[dbo\].\[$2\]/g;
    print $line;
}

close( FILE );
```

How It Works

The usefulness of this expression comes from the negative look-ahead, (?!, that allows the expression to check to make sure there isn't already an existing owner. If there isn't, the expression makes the replacement. The owner's name can be wrapped in brackets or not, and for the purposes of this expression you can assume the database restricts the characters in an owner's name to word characters.

The main part of the expression that contains this logic is as follows:

(?!	the beginning of a negative look-ahead . . .
\[	a literal left bracket . . .
?	found zero or one time . . .
\w	a word character . . .
+	found one or more times . . .
\]	a literal right bracket . . .
?	found zero or one time . . .

\.   a literal period (.) . . .

)   the end of the negative look-ahead.

This looks for a user, and if it finds it, the expression doesn't match and no replacement is made. The expression is prevented from adding owners to objects where it has already found an owner.

PHP

```
<html>
<head><title>6-13 Setting a SQL owner</title></head>
<body>
<form action="recipe6-13.php" method="post">
<input type="text" name="str"
        value="<?php print $_POST['str'];?>" /><br />
<input type="submit" value="Set Owner" /><br /><br />
<?php
if ( $_SERVER['REQUEST_METHOD'] == "POST" )
{
    $str = $_POST['str'];
    $newstr = preg_replace( "/(CREATE\s+PROCEDURE\s+)(?!\[?[A-Z]+\]?\.)(\w+)/i",
"$1[dbo].[$2]", $str );
    print $newstr;
}
?>
</form>
</body>
</html>
```

How It Works

See "How It Works" under the Perl example in this recipe for a breakdown of the expression.

Python

```
#!/usr/bin/python
import re
import sys

nargs = len(sys.argv)

if nargs > 1:

    myfile = sys.argv[1]
    output = open( myfile )
    regex = re.compile( r'(CREATE\s+PROCEDURE\s+)(?!\[?[A-Z]+\]?\.)(\w+)', re.I )
```

```
        lines = output.readlines()
        for line in lines:
            formatted = regex.sub( r'\1[dbo].[\2]', line )
            print formatted,

        output.close()

else:
    print 'Supply a parameter!',
```

How It Works

Look at "How It Works" under the Perl example in this recipe to see how this expression works.

Vim

```
:%s/\(CREATE\s\+PROCEDURE\s\+\)\%(\[\?[A-Z]\+\]\?\.\)\@!\(\w\+\)\c/\1[dbo].[\2]/
```

How It Works

At first, I was caught by the fact that the second group in the series, which isn't captured in PCRE expressions, was put back into the replacement expression as the back reference \2. I just changed the second group to start with \%(, which makes a group a noncapturing group. I also escaped all the (,), +, and ? characters.

The other two changes are the \@! sequence that modifies the expression preceding it to a negative look-ahead and the added \c at the end of the expression, which in Vim makes the expression ignore case.

6-14. Finding a Method Declaration

You can use this recipe to search for a method declaration in Java source code. In this
example, it looks for int MyMethod(), either public or private.

Perl

```perl
#!/usr/bin/perl -w
use strict;

my $fn = $ARGV[0] || die "Please supply a filename!";
open ( FILE, $ARGV[0] ) || die "Cannot open file.";

while (<FILE>)
{
    my $line = $_;
    print $line if ( $line =~ /^\s*(?:public|private)\s+int\s+MyMethod\s*\(/ );
}

close( FILE );
```

How It Works

The expression breaks down as follows:

^	the beginning of the line . . .
\s	whitespace . . .
*	found zero, one, or many times . . .
(?:	a noncapturing group that contains . . .
public	to find public declarations . . .
|	or . . .
private	to find private declarations . . .
)	the end of the noncapturing group
\s	whitespace . . .
+	one or more times . . .
int	i, n, and t . . .
\s	whitespace . . .
+	one or more times . . .
MyMethod	the name of the method . . .

\s   whitespace . . .

*   zero, one, or many times . . .

\(an opening parenthesis.

And the expression stops here, making the assumption that there's enough information here to locate the correct method declaration.

PHP

```
<html>
<head><title>6-14 Searching for method declarations</title></head>
<body>
<form action="recipe6-14.php" method="post">
<input type="text" name="str"
value="<?php print $_POST['str'];?>" /><br />
<input type="submit" value="Find variable declarations" /><br /><br />
<?php
if ( $_SERVER['REQUEST_METHOD'] == "POST" )
{
    $str = $_POST['str'];
    if ( preg_match( "/^\s*(?:public|private)\s+int\s+MyMethod\s*\(/", $str ) )
    {
        print "<b>Found declaration in:  '" .
            htmlspecialchars($str) . "'</b><br/>";
    }
    else
    {
        print "<b>Found no match in text:  '" .
            htmlspecialchars($str) . "'</b><br/>";
    }
}
?>
</form>
</body>
</html>
```

How It Works

See "How It Works" under the Perl example for information on how this expression works.

Shell Scripting

```
$ grep '^[[:space:]]*\(public\|private\)[[:space:]]\+int[[:space:]]\+⏎
MyMethod[[:space:]]*('filename
```

How It Works

The grep expression uses the [[:space:]] character class to match whitespace such as tabs and spaces. The (,), |, and + characters are escaped in the expression; otherwise it's put together the same way as the expression explained in "How It Works" under the Perl example in this recipe.

Vim

```
/^\s*\(public\|private\)\s\+int\s\+MyMethod\s*(
```

How It Works

See "How It Works" under the Perl example in this recipe, and remember to escape (,), |, and + to give them their "metacharacter status."

See Also 6-3, 6-4, 6-8

6-15. Changing Null Comparisons

You can use this recipe to swap null evaluations in tests. Some programming shops by convention write their null comparisons like this:

```
if ( null == myvar )
```

instead of like this:

```
if ( myvar == null )
```

This recipe will make the latter look like the former. The reason why some programmers use this convention is to avoid accidentally assigning a value to null by using = instead of == in the comparison. The compiler will produce an error if the code looks like this:

```
if ( null = myvar )
```

But it won't necessarily produce an error if the code looks like this:

```
if ( myvar = null )
```

■**Note** This expression was written to handle basic comparisons. Its limitations don't allow it to work with comparisons such as if ((x * 3) = null).

Perl

```perl
#!/usr/bin/perl -w
use strict;

open ( FILE, $ARGV[0] ) || die "Cannot open file!";
while (<FILE>)
{
    my $line = $_;
    $line =~ s/\(\s*(\w+)\s* ([=!]?=)\s*null\s*\)/( null $2 $1 )/g;
    print $line;
}

close( FILE );
```

How It Works

Two groups in this expression capture the comparison operator and the variable name, respectively. The word *null* isn't important to capture because you can put it back into the replacement expression. The search expression is as follows:

\(	an open parenthesis . . .
\s	whitespace . . .
*	found zero, one, or many times . . .
(	a group that contains . . .
\w	a word character . . .
+	found one or more times . . .
)	the end of the group . . .
\s	whitespace . . .
*	found zero or more times . . .
(	a second group . . .
[	a character class that can contain . . .
!	an exclamation point . . .
=	an equal sign . . .
]	the end of the character class . . .
?	that may appear one time . . .
=	a second equal sign . . .
)	the end of the second group . . .
\s	whitespace . . .
*	found zero or more times . . .
null	the word *null* . . .
\s	whitespace . . .
*	zero, one, or many times . . .
\)	the closing parenthesis.

The first group will capture the comparison operator, which can be either != or ==. This needs to be captured in a group because it can vary among matches. Since the character class is qualified with a ?, which will make the character class optional, the group will also capture assignments that include a single =.

The second group is the variable name itself, which is put back into the replacement expression with the second back reference $2.

PHP

```
<html>
<head><title>6-15 Changing null comparisons</title></head>
<body>
<form action="recipe6-15.php" method="post">
<input type="text" name="str"
value="<?php print $_POST['str'];?>" /><br />
<input type="submit" value="Change null comparisons" /><br /><br />
<?php
if ( $_SERVER['REQUEST_METHOD'] == "POST" )
{
    $str = $_POST['str'];
    $newstr = preg_replace( "/\(\s*(\w+)\s*([=!]?=)\s*null\s*\)/",
        "( null $2 $1 )", $str );
    print "<b>Original text was:  '" .
        htmlspecialchars($str) . "'</b><br/>";
    print "<b>New text is:  '" . htmlspecialchars($newstr) . "'</b><br/>";
}
?>
</form>
</body>
</html>
```

How It Works

See "How It Works" under the Perl example in this recipe.

Shell Scripting

```
$ sed 's/( *\([a-z0-9_]\+\) *\([=!]\?=\) *null *)/( null \2 \1 )/g' filename
```

How It Works

Instead of using the \s character class, this sed example uses a space.

This example also shows how to use the longer character class [a-z0-9_] when the shorthand \w isn't available.

Vim

```
:%s/(\s*\(\w\+\)\s*\([=!]\?=\)\s*null\s*)/( null \2 \1 )/g
```

How It Works

See "How It Works" under the Perl recipe, and remember to escape (,), and +.

6-16. Changing DOS Text to Unix Text

You can use this recipe to replace DOS end-of-line combinations with Unix end-of-line characters.

Perl

```perl
#!/usr/bin/perl -w
use strict;

open ( FILE, $ARGV[0] ) || die "Cannot open file!";
while (<FILE>)
{
    my $line = $_;
    if ( $line =~ s/\r//g )
    {
        print $line;
    }
}

close( FILE );
```

How It Works

Windows text files have extra line characters at the end of the line, and this can sometimes cause problems on a Unix or Linux box. This can especially rear its ugly head when a text file is transferred as binary over an FTP session. (ASCII mode on most FTP servers takes the extra line terminator out during transfer.) This can cause issues with shell scripts, and so on.

This simple recipe will remove the extra character, which is simply this: \r. It's removed here by replacing it with a zero-length string.

Note A really useful command-line utility included with many Linux distributions and Unix operating systems is the od command. When used with the -c parameter, the od command will print all the characters in output. You can use a pipe (|) to filter the output of any of these scripts through od -c to see the results: ./myscript.py data | od -c, where myscript.py contains the code in this recipe.

Python

```python
#!/usr/bin/python
import re
import sys

nargs = len(sys.argv)
if nargs > 1:
```

```
    myfile = sys.argv[1]
output = open( myfile )

regex = re.compile( r'\r' )
lines = output.readlines()
for line in lines:
    formatted = regex.sub( r'', line )
    print formatted,

output.close()
else:
    print 'I\'ve seen Tron eight times',
```

How It Works

To learn more about how this recipe works, see "How It Works" under the Perl example.

Vim

```
%s/^M//g
```

How It Works

In the previous Vim example, ^M represents the Ctrl+M sequence. It's put into the command by pressing Ctrl+V first, then pressing Ctrl+M, and then typing in the rest of the expression.

6-17. Searching for a Subject in Mail Files

This recipe is a simple expression that you can use to search for subject lines in mail files.

■**Note** Mail files can be in several different locations, depending on the environment you're using. Common locations are `/var/spool/mail/$USER`, `$HOME/mail`, and `$HOME/mbox` on *nix systems.

Perl

```
#!/usr/bin/perl -w
use strict;

open ( FILE, $ARGV[0] ) || die "Cannot open file!";
while (<FILE>)
{
    my $line = $_;
    print $line if ( $line =~ /^[ >]*Subject:/ );
}

close( FILE );
```

How It Works

This expression uses a character class to find subjects that may be in forwarded mails or replied-to mails, as well as incoming items. You can use this script against a mailbox file that most POP3 clients create.

^	the beginning of the line . . .
[	a character class that contains . . .
<space>	a space . . .
>	a > . . .
]	the end of the character class . . .
*	zero, one, or many times . . .
Subject:	the subject label.

Variations on this expression allow you to search for recipients, senders, and dates.

PHP

```
<html>
<head><title>6-17 Searching for a subject in mail files</title></head>
<body>
<form action="recipe6-17.php" method="post">
<input type="submit" value="Parse log" /><br/><br/>
<?php
if ( $_SERVER['REQUEST_METHOD'] == "POST" )
{

    $myfile = @fopen( "/path/to/mailfile", "r" )
        or die ("Cannot open file $myfile");

    while ( $line = @fgets( $myfile, 1024 ) )
    {
        if ( preg_match( "/^[ >]*Subject:/", $line ) )
        {
            echo $line . "<br />";
        }
    }
    fclose($myfile);
}
?>
</form>
</body>
</html>
```

How It Works

For details about this expression, see "How It Works" under the Perl example in this recipe.

Python

```
#!/usr/bin/python
import re
import sys
from os import popen

nargs = len(sys.argv)
if nargs > 1:
    myfile = sys.argv[1]
    output = open( myfile )
    regex = re.compile( r'^[ >]*Subject:' )

    lines = output.readlines()
    for line in lines:
        if regex.match( line ):
            print line,
    output.close()
else:
    print 'Please supply a parameter!',
```

How It Works

To see why this expression works, see "How It Works" under the Perl example.

6-18. Formatting BIND Configuration Files

This recipe allows you to format host and alias entries (A and CNAME, respectively) in Berkeley Internet Name Domain (BIND) configuration files. If some entries have spaces instead of tabs, or multiple spaces or tabs, this recipe will reformat the lines to have a single tab between parts of an entry. This recipe handles the forward lookup files.

Here's an example of the configuration file I used when testing this expression:

```
@        IN      SOA     host.example.com.        root@example.com        (
                                 17 ; serial
                                 28800 ; refresh
                                 14400 ; retry
                                 3600000 ; expire
                                 86400 ; ttl
                                 )



         IN      NS      ns1.example.com.

host1      IN      A       10.0.0.1
host2 IN CNAME    host1.example.com.
```

Perl

```perl
#!/usr/bin/perl -w
use strict;

open ( FILE, $ARGV[0] ) || die "Cannot open file!";
while (<FILE>)
{
    my $line = $_;
    $line =~ s/^([A-Za-z0-9][-A-Za-z0-9]+)\s+(IN)\s+(A|CNAME)\s+([A-Za-z0-9]↵
[-A-Za-z0-9.]+\.|[\d.]+)$/$1\t$2\t$3\t$4/;
    print $line;
}

close( FILE );
```

How It Works

This expression consists of a four groups, each separated by the \s+ expression, which matches one or more whitespace character (tabs, spaces).

The first group is ([A-Za-z0-9][-A-Za-z0-9]+), which matches a hostname. Hostnames must start with a letter or number and after that can include also a hyphen (for example, host and my-host but not -host).

The second group matches IN, and the third group matches either A or CNAME.

The fourth group in the expression matches either a hostname (with ([A-Za-z0-9][-A-Za-z0-9]+)) or an Internet Protocol (IP) address (with [\d.]+). I'm not checking for a valid IP address in this expression for brevity, but if you're interested in how to validate IP addresses, see recipe 4-10.

Python

```
#!/usr/bin/python
import re
import sys
from os import popen

nargs = len(sys.argv)
if nargs > 1:
    myfile = sys.argv[1]
    output = open( myfile )
    regex = re.compile( r'^([A-Za-z0-9][-A-Za-z0-9]+)\s+(IN)\s+(A|CNAME)\s+↩
([A-Za-z0-9][-A-Za-z0-9.]+\.|[\d.]+)$' )
    lines = output.readlines()
    for line in lines:
        formatted = regex.sub( r'\1\t\2\t\3\t\4', line )
        print formatted,
    output.close()
else:
    print 'Please supply a parameter!'
```

How It Works

For details about how this regular expression works, see "How It Works" under the Perl example.

See Also 4-10

6-19. Parsing the Output of df

This simple recipe filters the output of df to print only drives that have capacity greater than 50 percent.

Perl

```
#!/usr/bin/perl
use strict;

while ( <STDIN> )
{
    print $_ if ( /\s(([5-9][0-9])|(100))\%\s/ );
}
```

How It Works

This recipe simply looks for a percentage figure greater than 50 and prints matching lines. It's relevant because more than likely neither the mount point nor the disk path is a percentage.

The expression is as follows:

\s	whitespace . . .
(	a group that contains . . .
(	another group with . . .
[5-9]	five through nine (in the tens place) . . .
[0-9]	zero through nine (in the ones place) . . .
)	the end of the group . . .
|	or . . .
100	1, 0, and 0 . . .
)	the end of the group . . .
\%	a percent sign . . .
\s	whitespace.

Catching five through nine in the tens place and one through nine in the ones place will catch anything between 50 and 99. You catch 100 by using 100—there's no need for a fancier expression.

PHP

```
<html>
<head><title>6-19 parsing the output of df</title></head>
<body>
<form action="recipe6-19.php" method="post">
<input type="submit" value="Find more than half full drives" /><br /><br />
<?php
if ( $_SERVER['REQUEST_METHOD'] == "POST" )
{
    $ps = popen( 'df', 'r' );
    while ( $stuff = fgets( $ps, 2056 ) )
    {
        $output .= $stuff;
    }

    $lines = explode( "\n", $output );

    foreach ( $lines as $line )
    {
        if ( preg_match( "/\s(([5-9][0-9])|(100))%\s/", $line ) )
        {
            print "<b>$line</b><br/>";
        }
    }

    pclose($ps);
}
?>
</form>
</body>
</html>
```

How It Works

See "How It Works" under the Perl example for an explanation of this expression.

Python

```
#!/usr/bin/python
import re
from os import popen

output = popen( 'df' )
regex = re.compile( r'^.*\s(([5-9][0-9])|(100))%\s.*$' )
```

```
lines = output.readlines()

for line in lines:
    if regex.match( line ):
        print line,

output.close()
```

How It Works

For an explanation of this expression, see "How It Works" under the Perl example in this recipe.

Shell Scripting

```
$ df | grep '\(\([5-9][0-9]\)\|\(100\)\)%'
```

How It Works

The previous grep example demonstrates running the df command and filtering its output through grep.

For a closer look at the expression, see "How It Works" under the Perl example in this recipe.

■ **See Also** 2-1, 4-3, 4-10, 4-17, 6-12

6-20. Parsing Apache Log Files

You can use this recipe to format entries in Apache access files with a 404 error in the line.
It will print the name of the file that a user attempted to retrieve, as well as the IP address that
was the source of the request.

Perl

```perl
#!/usr/bin/perl -w
use strict;

open ( FILE, $ARGV[0] ) || die "Cannot open file!";
while (<FILE>)
{
    my $line = $_;
    if ( $line =~ s/^([\d.]*?)\s.*GET\s(\/\S*)\sHTTP\/\d\.\d\"\s↵
404\s\d{3}$/$1:  $2/g )
    {
        print $line;
    }
}

close( FILE );
```

How It Works

The Perl script prints the line only if a replacement was made. Since 404 is specified in the
search string, only entries with 404 errors in them will be formatted and printed to the screen.
The expression's other main purpose is to grab the IP address and the filename from the entry.

The IP address expression isn't the full IP address validation expression because this is an
entry written by Apache as visitors come to the site, so there shouldn't be any cases where the
address is an invalid address.

The following is a more detailed look at the entire expression:

^	the beginning of the line . . .
(	a group that contains . . .
[	a character class that matches . . .
\d	a digit . . .
.	or a dot . . .
]	the end of the character class . . .
*?	as many times as necessary, up to . . .
)	the end of the group . . .
\s	whitespace . . .

*	found zero, one, or many times . . .
.	any character . . .
*	up to . . .
GET	G, E, T . . .
\s	whitespace . . .
(	a group that contains . . .
\/	a slash (to start the filename) . . .
\S	a nonspace character . . .
*	found zero, one, or many times . . .
)	the end of the group . . .
\s	whitespace . . .
HTTP	H, T, T, and P . . .
\/	a slash . . .
\d	a digit . . .
\.	a period . . .
\d	another digit . . .
\"	a double quote . . .
\s	whitespace . . .
404	4, 0, 4 . . .
\s	whitespace . . .
\d	a digit . . .
{3}	found three times . . .
$	the end of the line.

This expression does some checking to make sure the 404 error is in the right place and that the match isn't occurring on a file called 404.html or something similar. That's why the expression gets more specific around the end. The first group is the IP address and is put into the replacement expression by the back reference $1, and the second group is the filename and is referenced by $2.

PHP

```
<html>
<head><title>6-20 Parsing Apache log files</title></head>
<body>
<form action="recipe6-20.php" method="post">
<input type="submit" value="Parse log" /><br/><br/>
<?php
if ( $_SERVER['REQUEST_METHOD'] == "POST" )
{

    $myfile = @fopen( "/private/var/log/httpd/access_log", "r" )
        or die ("Cannot open file $myfile");

    while ( $line = @fgets( $myfile, 1024 ) )
    {
        if ( preg_match( "/^([\d.]*?)\s.*GET\s(\/\S*)\sHTTP\/\d\.\d\"\s/↵
404\s\d{3}$/", $line ) )
        {
            $newstr = preg_replace( "/^([\d.]*?)\s.*GET\s(\/\S*)\s↵
HTTP\/\d\.\d\"\s404\s\d{3}$/", "$1:$2", $line );
            echo $newstr . "<br />";
        }
    }
    fclose($myfile);
}
?>
</form>
</body>
</html>
```

How It Works

To see how this expression works in detail, see "How It Works" under the Perl example in this recipe.

Python

```
#!/usr/bin/python
import re
import sys

nargs = len(sys.argv)
if nargs > 1:
    myfile = sys.argv[1]
    output = open( myfile )
    regex = re.compile( r'^([\d.]*?)\s.*GET\s(\/\S*)\sHTTP\/\d\.\d\"\s404\s\d{3}$' )
```

```
    lines = output.readlines()
    for line in lines:
        if regex.match( line ):
            formatted = regex.sub( r'\1:  \2', line )
            print formatted,
    output.close()
else:
    print 'One ping.  One ping, only . . .',
```

How It Works

To see how this expression breaks down, refer to "How It Works" under the Perl example.

▓**See Also** 6-17, 6-18, 6-21

6-21. Parsing Unix syslog Files

You can use this recipe to find out what the local IP address is when assigned by pppd by tailing a log and watching out for output from pppd.

I don't show a PHP example here because allowing a PHP script to open a syslog file would require giving read access to the log file to the Web server. This isn't a good idea for security reasons. However, if you're curious, the expression would be identical to the Perl example.

Perl

```
#!/usr/bin/perl -w
use strict;

open ( FILE, $ARGV[0] ) || die "Cannot open file!";
while (<FILE>)
{
    my $line = $_;
    # Jul 25 10:30:09 rhes-pe2400-01 pppd[1396]: local  IP address 209.98.170.206
    if ( $line =~ s/^.+\s+pppd\[\d+\]:\s+local\s+IP\s+address\s+([\d.]+)$/$1/ )
    {
        print $line;
    }
}

close( FILE );
```

How It Works

This expression searches for output from pppd that lists the local IP address. You can use this expression to capture new interface IP addresses on a system that dials up to the Internet.

The expression searches for pppd with ^.+pppd\[\d+\]:, which works because in the log entry (shown in the comments above the expression), the name of the command precedes a process identifier (PID) in brackets. Getting this detailed may not be necessary, but it adds an extra measure that the IP address is coming from pppd in case the message "local IP address" is printed by a different command.

The words *local IP address* are separated by spaces, but, as shown by the log entry, the spaces are inconsistent. You can address this issue by using \s+ to match one or more white-space (tab or space).

The last part of the expression, ([\d.]+)$, is as follows:

(a group that contains . . .

[a character class that matches . . .

\d   a digit . . .

.   a period . . .

]	the end of the character class . . .
+	one or more times . . .
)	the end of the group . . .
$	end of the line.

This is the expression that will actually match the IP address that can be referenced with the $1 back reference.

Python

```
#!/usr/bin/python
import re
import sys

nargs = len(sys.argv)
if nargs > 1:
    myfile = sys.argv[1]
    output = open( myfile )
    regex = re.compile( r'^.+\s+pppd\[\d+\]:\s+local\s+IP\s+address\s+([\d.]+)$' )
    lines = output.readlines()
    for line in lines:
        if regex.match( line ):
            formatted = regex.sub( r'Local IP Address is:  \1', line )
            print formatted,
    output.close()
else:
    print 'Please supply a parameter!',
```

How It Works

For details on how this expression works, see "How It Works" under the Perl example.

___

See Also 6-17, 6-18, 6-20, 6-22
___

6-22. Parsing INI Files

This recipe demonstrates an easy way of parsing keys and values in INI files. Given a key/value pair such as "foo=bar", this expression will grab foo as the key and bar as the value.

Perl

```
#!/usr/bin/perl -w
use strict;

my $fn = $ARGV[0] || die "Please supply a parameter\n";
open( FILE, $fn ) || die "Could not open file\n";
while ( <FILE> )
{
print $_ if ( s/^([^=]+?)=\s*(.*)$/Key: '$1'; Value: '$2'/ );
}

close( FILE );
```

How It Works

The expression that's used to grab the key is ^([^=]+?). It isn't concerned about what type of character is in a key, just as long as it isn't an equal sign (=). It will grab everything up to the first equal sign with the help of +?, which is a lazy or conservative qualifier that stops as soon as it can (which in this case is at the first =).

The matching expression, broken down, is as follows:

^	the beginning of the line . . .
(	a group that contains . . .
[^	a character class that doesn't contain . . .
=	an equal sign . . .
]	the end of the character class . . .
+?	found one or more times, up to the first . . .
)	the end of the group . . .
=	equal sign . . .
\s	whitespace . . .
*	found zero or more times . . .
(	a group that captures . . .
.	any character . . .

> *   any number of times (including none) . . .
>
>)   the end of the group . . .
>
> $ the end of the line.

The second group, (.*), matches everything after the first equal sign. This will contain the value of the key/value INI entry.

PHP

```
<html>
<head><title>6-22 Parsing INI Files</title></head>
<body>
<form action="recipe6-22.php" method="post">
<input type="text" name="str"
    value="<?php print $_POST['str'];?>" /><br />
<input type="submit" value="Parse INI entry" /><br /><br />
<?php
if ( $_SERVER['REQUEST_METHOD'] == "POST" )
{
    $str = $_POST['str'];
    $newstr = preg_replace( "/^([^=]+?)=\s*(.*)$/",
        "Key: '$1'; Value: '$2'", $str );
    print "<b>Parsed text is:  '" .
        htmlspecialchars($newstr) . "'</b><br/>";
}
?>
</form>
</body>
</html>
```

How It Works

See "How It Works" under the Perl example in this recipe for an explanation of this expression.

Python

```
#!/usr/bin/python
import re
import sys

nargs = len(sys.argv)
if nargs > 1:
    myfile = sys.argv[1]
    output = open( myfile )
    regex = re.compile( r'^([^=]+?)=\s*(.*)' )

    lines = output.readlines()
    for line in lines:
        if regex.match( line ):
            formatted = regex.sub( r'Value is "\2" for key "\1"', line )
            print formatted,
    output.close()
else:
    print 'Please supply a parameter!',
```

How It Works

For information about how this expression does the trick, see "How It Works" under the Perl example.

Index

$ *line anchor—the end of the line*

1-1, 1-9, 1-13, 1-20, 1-27, 2-2, 2-3, 2-4, 2-6, 2-7, 2-8, 2-10, 2-11, 2-12, 2-13, 2-14, 3-1, 3-2, 3-3, 3-4, 3-5, 3-6, 4-1, 4-2, 4-3, 4-5, 4-7, 4-8, 4-9, 4-10, 4-11, 4-12, 4-13, 4-14, 4-15, 4-16, 4-17, 4-18, 4-19, 4-20, 4-21, 4-23, 6-2, 6-10, 6-12, 6-18, 6-20, 6-21, 6-22

^   *line anchor—the beginning of the line*

1-1, 1-9, 1-12, 1-17, 1-18, 1-21, 2-2, 2-3, 2-4, 2-5, 2-6, 2-7, 2-8, 2-10, 2-11, 2-12, 2-13, 2-14, 2-15, 3-1, 3-2, 3-5, 3-6, 4-1, 4-2, 4-3, 4-5, 4-6, 4-7, 4-8, 4-9, 4-10, 4-11, 4-12, 4-13, 4-14, 4-15, 4-16, 4-17, 4-18, 4-19, 4-20, 4-21, 4-22, 4-23, 6-1, 6-2, 6-6, 6-7, 6-8, 6-9, 6-10, 6-11, 6-12, 6-14, 6-17, 6-18, 6-20, 6-21, 6-22

*   *qualifier—zero or more*

1-1, 1-7, 1-9, 1-15, 1-17, 1-25, 1-27, 2-2, 2-3, 2-4, 2-6, 3-1, 3-3, 3-4, 3-5, 3-6, 4-19, 4-20, 4-21, 5-4, 5-5, 6-1, 6-2, 6-3, 6-4, 6-8, 6-9, 6-10, 6-11, 6-12, 6-14, 6-15, 6-17, 6-20, 6-22

(...)   *expression group—captures matches and allows qualifiers and ranges to be applied to a group of expressions*

1-3, 1-4, 1-10, 1-14, 1-16, 1-18, 2-1, 2-2, 2-3, 2-4, 2-5, 2-6, 2-7, 2-8, 2-9, 2-10, 2-12, 2-15, 3-1, 3-2, 3-3, 3-5, 3-6, 4-1, 4-2, 4-4, 4-5, 4-6, 4-10, 4-11, 4-15, 4-17, 4-19, 4-20, 4-21, 5-1, 5-3, 5-4, 5-7, 6-1, 6-2, 6-3, 6-8, 6-10, 6-11, 6-12, 6-15, 6-18, 6-19, 6-20, 6-21, 6-22

-      *can specify a range inside a character class (see [ ])*

1-9, 1-14, 2-1, 2-5, 2-10, 2-11, 2-12, 2-13, 2-14, 2-15, 4-3, 4-7, 4-8, 4-10, 4-11, 4-12, 4-14, 4-15, 4-16, 4-17, 4-21, 6-12, 6-18, 6-19

+   *qualifier—one or more*

1-3, 1-10, 1-11, 1-14, 1-15, 2-3, 2-4, 2-6, 2-7, 2-8, 2-9, 2-10, 2-11, 2-12, 2-13, 2-14, 3-1, 3-2, 3-6, 4-4, 4-5, 4-7, 4-8, 4-11, 4-12, 4-19, 4-20, 4-21, 5-1, 5-2, 5-3, 5-4, 5-5, 5-7, 6-3, 6-8, 6-10, 6-11, 6-12, 6-13, 6-14, 6-15, 6-18, 6-21

{}   *range qualifier—specifies numbers of occurrences for previous expression*

1-9, 2-8, 2-13, 2-14, 2-15, 3-1, 3-2, 4-1, 4-2, 4-3, 4-4, 4-9, 4-10, 4-11, 4-12, 4-13, 4-14, 4-15, 4-16, 4-18, 4-20, 6-12, 6-20

forums.apress.com

FOR PROFESSIONALS BY PROFESSIONALS™

JOIN THE APRESS FORUMS AND BE PART OF OUR COMMUNITY. You'll find discussions that cover topics of interest to IT professionals, programmers, and enthusiasts just like you. If you post a query to one of our forums, you can expect that some of the best minds in the business—especially Apress authors, who all write with *The Expert's Voice*™—will chime in to help you. Why not aim to become one of our most valuable participants (MVPs) and win cool stuff? Here's a sampling of what you'll find:

DATABASES

Data drives everything.

Share information, exchange ideas, and discuss any database programming or administration issues.

INTERNET TECHNOLOGIES AND NETWORKING

Try living without plumbing (and eventually IPv6).

Talk about networking topics including protocols, design, administration, wireless, wired, storage, backup, certifications, trends, and new technologies.

JAVA

We've come a long way from the old Oak tree.

Hang out and discuss Java in whatever flavor you choose: J2SE, J2EE, J2ME, Jakarta, and so on.

MAC OS X

All about the Zen of OS X.

OS X is both the present and the future for Mac apps. Make suggestions, offer up ideas, or boast about your new hardware.

OPEN SOURCE

Source code is good; understanding (open) source is better.

Discuss open source technologies and related topics such as PHP, MySQL, Linux, Perl, Apache, Python, and more.

PROGRAMMING/BUSINESS

Unfortunately, it is.

Talk about the Apress line of books that cover software methodology, best practices, and how programmers interact with the "suits."

WEB DEVELOPMENT/DESIGN

Ugly doesn't cut it anymore, and CGI is absurd.

Help is in sight for your site. Find design solutions for your projects and get ideas for building an interactive Web site.

SECURITY

Lots of bad guys out there—the good guys need help.

Discuss computer and network security issues here. Just don't let anyone else know the answers!

TECHNOLOGY IN ACTION

Cool things. Fun things.

It's after hours. It's time to play. Whether you're into LEGO® MINDSTORMS™ or turning an old PC into a DVR, this is where technology turns into fun.

WINDOWS

No defenestration here.

Ask questions about all aspects of Windows programming, get help on Microsoft technologies covered in Apress books, or provide feedback on any Apress Windows book.

HOW TO PARTICIPATE:

Go to the Apress Forums site at **http://forums.apress.com/**.

Click the New User link.